YOUNG VOICES FROM WILD MILWAUKEE

The Urban Ecology Center and Me

The gateway to Milwaukee Rotary Centennial Arboretum
at Riverside Park Urban Ecology Center branch
(Photo courtesy of Matt Flower)

ALSO BY GAIL GRENIER

Calling All Horses
Dog Woman
Don't Worry Baby
Dessert First

Gail shares profits from the sales of these four books with HOPE Network, the charity she founded in 1982.

Young Voices from Wild Milwaukee

The Urban Ecology Center and Me

Stories Gathered by

Gail Grenier

HenschelHAUS Publishing, Inc.
Milwaukee, Wisconsin

Published by HenschelHAUS Publishing, Inc.
2625 S. Greeley St. Suite 201
Milwaukee, WI 53207
www.henschelhausbooks.com

ISBN: 978159598-609-2
E-ISBN: 978159598-610-8
LCCN: 2018936031

Printed by Paragon Printing and Graphics, Milwaukee, WI

For the people of Milwaukee, Wisconsin

With gratitude to Mike Larson,
the guardian angel of this book

Thanks also and always to Karen Cluppert,
my guide to art and technology

Kids running into woods, Riverside Park
(Photo courtesy of Taylor Chobanian)

"Never doubt that a small group of thoughtful, committed citizens can change the world; indeed, it's the only thing that ever has."
—Margaret Mead

Profits from the sale of *Young Voices from Wild Milwaukee* will be shared with the Urban Ecology Center.

Acknowledgment

My deepest gratitude goes to Milwaukee's Urban Ecology Center, a jewel hidden in plain sight. Thank you, UEC staff, for your patience and support during four years of my questions. And thank you for being there for all of us.

TABLE OF CONTENTS

[The storytellers often refer to Urban Ecology Center
staff members. Here is a list of those people and
how they have served at the UEC.]

The Stories

[Numbers indicate the age of each storyteller
at the time of the interview.]

BY WAY OF INTRODUCTION

BEFORE YOU LOOK INSIDE THESE PAGES

Young Voices from Wild Milwaukee is about finding nature in the city.

If you're curious about the world outside, *Young Voices from Wild Milwaukee* is for you. In this book, you'll find true stories about the power of nature ... and about the power of a nature center. The stories are for every reader of every age.

Here are fifteen chapters made of real words spoken by people ages fifteen through forty. They come from different neighborhoods and they look at the world in different ways. But all the storytellers have one thing in common: *nature has changed their lives.*

Each person featured in *Young Voices from Wild Milwaukee* speaks from the heart. No story is the same; the accounts are funny, touching, long, short, sad ... and all true.

Reading *Young Voices from Wild Milwaukee* is like walking through a flower garden. Just as you would pick certain flowers you like, you might prefer certain sections of the book. It's all here:

- How people fell in love with nature and with a place ...
- How nature changed them at various ages ...

YOUNG VOICES FROM WILD MILWAUKEE

- How a nature center transformed urban youth into leaders …

- How a nature center changed a high-crime neighborhood …

- How workers show they care about others, on the job and in the neighborhood…

- How people young and old become mentors for each other …

- And how amazing and funny animals can be.

The people whose voices you hear in this book come from neighborhoods in and around Milwaukee, Wisconsin. The nature center they love is Milwaukee's Urban Ecology Center (UEC). It doesn't matter if you live in Milwaukee or any other place in this big, beautiful world; in *Young Voices from Wild Milwaukee*, you'll discover ideas you can bring to your own life.

… And if, on the way, you meet a strange word, you'll find a glossary at the end of the book.

~Gail Grenier, Story Gatherer

How the Stories Came to Be

Here's what I did, over a period starting in 2014 and lasting into 2017:

1. Asked the Urban Ecology Center for the names of people to interview.

2. Set up interview times and places.

3. Met with the storytellers; asked planned questions while running a tape recorder.

4. Re-spooled the tape when it got stuck in the tape recorder.

5. Asked unplanned questions.

6. Typed up the interviews word-for-word, using a transcription machine.

7. Removed my questions from interviews; left only the words of the storytellers.

8. Gave up on the tape recorder after another tape "injury" and my own personal injury from repetitive motion pressing the transcription machine foot pedal.

9. Finished the interviews using pen and paper.

10. Asked the storytellers for photos.

11. Gave printed interviews to the storytellers for their additions, corrections, and approval.

12. Repeated Number 11 as needed.

People speak differently from the way they write. Because this is an oral account and not written … and because I deleted my own questions from the accounts … you'll find that some of the stories jump from topic to topic. That's how conversations go. But all the speakers continue a train of thought that is vital to them.

Here is a list of my planned questions; the interviews meandered *a lot* from there:

- Describe a typical day in your life before the Urban Ecology Center became a part of your world.
- How did you discover the Urban Ecology Center (or how did the UEC discover you)?
- How did you get your love of nature?
- What did you do with the Urban Ecology Center?
- What was your favorite thing you did there?
- Did any of your friends also do things at the UEC?
- What would you say to other young people about the Center?
- How has your life changed because of the Urban Ecology Center?
- What do you think nature can do for young people's lives, in general?
- What would you tell a young person about the value of nature?
- Do you plan to be involved with the UEC in the future?
- What is your wish for the Urban Ecology Center?
- What is your wish for our world?

~Gail Grenier

FOREWORD

THE STORIES IN THIS BOOK: *ASTOUNDING!*

Mike Larson,
Visitor Services Manager at the Urban Ecology Center

I first walked in to the Urban Ecology Center in 2001, back when it was just a trailer behind a high school. At the time, I was an undergraduate in college. As a volunteer, I remember thinking the Urban Ecology Center was a nice little start-up organization whose enthusiastic staff made up for its apparent lack of resources. A staff member pulled me aside one day to show me some "plans"—architectural mock-ups for a future Urban Ecology Center building that was going to be built "over by those tennis courts someday." I remember looking around at the cluttered educational space with its leaky roof and second-hand aquariums and thinking to myself, "*Good luck, buddy.*"

THEY REALLY DID IT!

Five years later, I was invited to the grand opening of the brand-new Urban Ecology Center building in Riverside Park, a beautiful state-of-the-art green facility that was built with a variety of recycled and sustainable building materials, a slide for an entryway, and toilets that flushed with rain water.

*Mike Larson, Visitor Services Manager at the Urban Ecology Center
This photo was taken when Mike was leading an eco-travel trip to
Maine for the Urban Ecology Center. Penobscot Bay, Maine
(Photo courtesy of Mike Larson)*

Photovoltaic cells and a three-story rock climbing wall would soon follow. Looking around at the high ceilings, large windows and green roof garden, I couldn't help but be impressed with the little organization I had met in the trailer years before. My first astonished thought was, "Wow, they really did it!" followed closely by "Gee, I really wish I could work here!"

It wasn't until I was hired in 2007 that I learned the full story of the Urban Ecology Center. Its location behind the high school in Riverside Park was no accident. The historical park was one in a set of three designed at the end of the nineteenth century by Frederick Law Olmsted, famous for designing Central Park in New York City. At the turn of the twentieth century, Riverside Park was in its heyday, attracting hundreds of neighbors each week for horse-drawn carriage rides, picnics and leisure time with the family.

A dam on the Milwaukee River at North Avenue created ideal conditions for fishing, swimming and canoeing in the summer and ice skating in the winter. Historic photographs reveal how beautiful and well-loved the park and river were during the early part of the twentieth century. Unfortunately, this golden era was not to last.

The dam, which was so instrumental in producing the lake-like conditions that made Riverside Park so attractive, was also instrumental in its downfall. Accumulated sewage and pollution behind the dam eventually poisoned the water, killing the fish and choking the ecosystem, making the river unfit for swimming and water sports. On its worst days, the river started to smell like a sewer, and as a result people stopped coming to the park.

Park service budgets were slashed, and the regular maintenance of lawns and park buildings couldn't be justified in a park without visitors. So, the infrastructure fell into disrepair and the lawns became overgrown. The park was bisected by train tracks, and a tunnel that provided access to the west end of the park and the river was filled in during the construction of a football field for the high school, essentially cutting off the wooded area from the park and seemingly sealing its fate. As can often happen with an isolated area, an active drug trade and violent crime found their way into the park. By 1986, the crime in Riverside Park and the surrounding neighborhood was twice the city average and officials began to discuss the

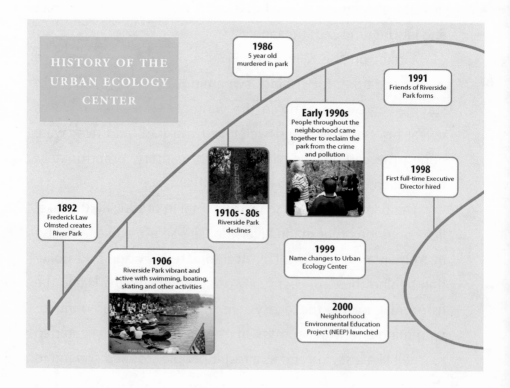

HISTORY OF THE
URBAN ECOLOGY
CENTER

1986
5 year old
murdered in park

1991
Friends of Riverside
Park forms

Early 1990s
People throughout the
neighborhood came
together to reclaim the
park from the crime
and pollution

1998
First full-time Executive
Director hired

1892
Frederick Law
Olmsted creates
River Park

1910s - 80s
Riverside Park
declines

1999
Name changes to Urban
Ecology Center

1906
Riverside Park vibrant and
active with swimming, boating,
skating and other activities

2000
Neighborhood
Environmental Education
Project (NEEP) launched

ultimate solution of razing the once proud park that had become a blight on the neighborhood.

OUTDOOR LABORATORY

A group of neighbors who objected to the idea of losing the park got together around a central idea: "The park is not the problem. Crime is the problem, and if we can solve the crime problem we can save the park." Sitting around the kitchen table of Else Ankel, one of the early catalysts of the Center, they organized several clean-up efforts in the park with neighborhood groups, scout troops, church groups and dozens of volunteers. They set to work removing mounds of trash that had accumulated in the park after years of neglect. They

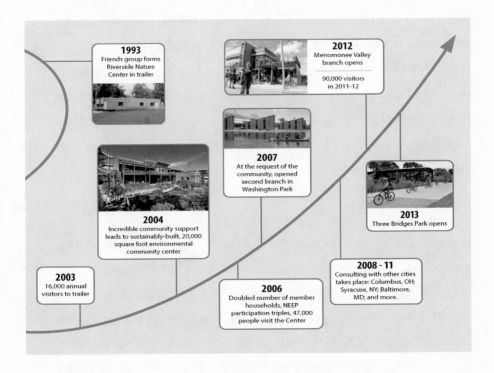

1993
Friends group forms Riverside Nature Center in trailer

2012
Menomonee Valley branch opens

90,000 visitors in 2011-12

2007
At the request of the community, opened second branch in Washington Park

2004
Incredible community support leads to sustainably-built, 20,000 square foot environmental community center

2013
Three Bridges Park opens

2003
16,000 annual visitors to trailer

2006
Doubled number of member households, NEEP participation triples, 47,000 people visit the Center

2008 - 11
Consulting with other cities takes place: Columbus, OH; Syracuse, NY; Baltimore, MD; and more.

scrubbed graffiti off of the trees. Still, cleaning the park wasn't enough. The neighbors knew that if they didn't do something to fill the park with people, things would return to the way they were before. Several ideas to activate the park were floated around, but the one that eventually stuck and took hold was a simple one: science education in an outdoor laboratory.

The laboratory had a lot of potential, but it needed a lot of work. Years of neglect had let the land in the forested area of the park go feral, overgrown with weeds and littered with fallen trees. However, since nobody had touched the park in years, its wildness gave it the potential to flourish with native plants and wildlife. Dead trees that are normally removed in most public parks were left standing where they became home for myriad species of fungus, algae, insects and birds that require such habitat to flourish. Through a grassroots effort, the park could realize its potential to have a remarkable biodiversity right in the heart of the city. The question arose: Wouldn't it be great if we could bring kids from schools nearby on field trips to Riverside Park, so they could learn in this remarkable outdoor laboratory? Thus, was born the idea that would become the Urban Ecology Center.

A SENSE OF SAFETY

It may seem counterintuitive, but bringing children into the park on a regular basis turned out to be a great way to fight crime. Drug dealers and other would-be criminals apparently found it less appealing to ply their trade where a bunch of third graders accompanied by an educator could come walking around the corner any minute. The sight of kids in the park also created a sense of safety in the neighborhood, and dog walkers and families started visiting Riverside with greater frequency. The more people that were using the park, the safer it became, which in turn attracted more people. The Urban Ecology Center started offering community programs on evenings and weekends, making the park even safer.

At the same time, a few other key improvements fell into place. The dam that had been the ultimate cause of pollution in the river upstream was removed and the polluted sediments above the dam were capped, allowing the water to become re-populated with fish and, eventually, anglers. The old train track that bisected the park was replaced with a bike path as part of the Rails to Trails program, making it more accessible to the community. The Milwaukee County Park System partnered with the Urban Ecology Center on trail maintenance, invasive plant removal and other land stewardship initiatives to clean up Riverside and increase its biodiversity. All of these factors lead to an upward spiral of positive improvement in the once blighted urban park. As the Center grew, so did the sense of well-being and hope in the community, and Riverside thrived.

CHANGE THE WORLD...ONE LIFE AT A TIME
Over the last twenty years, the Urban Ecology Center has continued to expand its reach and its positive impact on the City of Milwaukee. Today the Center operates in three urban parks, has been instrumental in adding dozens of acres of park land in urban centers that didn't exist before, has two state of the art "green" facilities with a third on the way and is directly

impacting more than 100,000 students, visitors and program participants each year. The breadth of the Center's reach is impressive, but it is the depth of the experience that many individuals have had with the Center that is the focus of this book. The testimonies of the folks interviewed for this work speak volumes about how a small group of caring citizens can change the world, one life at a time.

CONTACT WITH NATURE... AND A MENTOR

Early in the stages of the interviews that are the basis of this book, Gail Grenier had a working title of *How Nature Changed My Life*. However, as I read through the interviews, two unifying ideas caught my attention. The first was that while nature was certainly the backdrop in which these lives were changed, many of the interviewees pointed to specific people who were the catalysts of their transformation. Over and over again this theme becomes apparent: "How Erick Anderson changed my life... "How Jennifer Callaghan changed my life..." "How Terrance Davis changed my life..." Nature is only one of the magical ingredients in the Urban Ecology Center's recipe for individual and community transformation...the people are the other ingredient. This fits with what we know about the development of environmental consciousness in individuals.

The Urban Ecology Center educational model is based on research that identifies two factors that contribute to the development of an eco-centered lifestyle: consistent contact with nature as a child (our parks), and a mentor in the child's life who cared about the environment (our people). Each story in this book highlights the way these factors impacted each storyteller, and it is especially revealing to read how the mentors identified by some of the interviewees had mentors themselves in their own stories. It seems that the life-changing aspect of nature is a gift that is handed down generation to generation—sometimes across familial, cultural and socio-economic boundaries.

ASTOUNDING!

The second idea that unifies these stories can be summed up in one word: astounding. I can think of no better word that describes the impression left on people who experience the Urban Ecology Center for the first time. It is astounding that such beautiful natural areas and rich biodiversity can be found and preserved in the middle of Milwaukee. It is astounding that the Center lets its members borrow outdoor adventure equipment for canoe expectations, cross country ski outings and backpacking trips for free.

It is astounding what we can learn when we put the tools for research into the hands of young black and brown kids living in the heart of city, and they share their research with students, educators, and fellow researchers across the country. And, having worked here for nearly ten years, it is astounding to me that these experiences aren't more widespread. If only every neighborhood in every city could have an Urban Ecology Center. If only every student at an urban school had access to such wildness, such education, such first-hand experience. Think of the lives we could change.

"WE ARE HOME"
THESE STORIES HELPED
CHANGE MY LIFE

1958, City of Milwaukee, my neighborhood. I'm on the right.
My brother and my neighbor and I are sitting on a sewer cover, making mud pies.
That's Glendale Avenue behind us, before the concrete went in.

WEEDS, DIRT, SCRUBBY TREES, AND A BILLBOARD

Our northwest Milwaukee neighborhood was brand new when we moved there in 1956. We rode our balloon-tire bikes on soft dirt roads and hilly dirt alleyways. Sometimes the dirt became mud. We walked down the block to creeks where we picked sweet pea wildflowers, caught turtles, and experienced wild fears of quicksand. One spring, I found an abandoned baby rabbit whose eyes hadn't yet opened. I brought the little black creature home, put it in a shoebox padded with rags, and tried to keep it alive. That bunny gave me my first lesson about death.

It was the 1950s and there were scads of children. My brother and I and the neighbor kids roamed. As our neighborhood grew, we had some of our best fun playing in construction sites on evenings and weekends when workers were gone. We explored basements of homes that looked like giant matchstick creations. We clambered into the enormous buckets of "steam shovels." After one big rain, we floated a boat in a giant puddle; the boat was a cement hopper, I think.

Eventually, concrete workers invaded our block. When they went home for the evening, we had great fun climbing all over a mammoth street-making machine—it became a huge stage where we danced the Twist while our parents used 16-mm. cameras to make home movies of our performances. The workers eventually laid smooth sidewalks, curbs, alleys and streets. We found that we could ride our bikes faster on cement, but our falls were harder. My knees were scabbed and un-scabbed in turn over the span of entire summers.

Slowly the creeks disappeared—I still have no idea what happened to them. In their places sprouted single-family Cape Cods and ranch homes, four-family apartment buildings, a delicatessen, and a synagogue. At the end of all the construction, only one tiny vacant lot was left. It was there that I fell in love with nature, across the street from our home on the corner of West Beckett and Glendale Avenues. The lot had everything we needed: weeds, dirt, scrubby trees, and a billboard.

"WE ARE HOME."

The place was a haven for my brother Danny and me, and for all our friends in the neighborhood, all year 'round. In warm weather, we built forts in the scrubby trees. The boys were soldiers and they fought great battles. We girls were nurses who bandaged their wounds. On still winter evenings, guided by moonlight, Danny and I went sledding from the crest of the vacant lot down a tiny slope to the alley.

The billboard was the best part of our vacant lot. We climbed up to its platform and lay on our stomachs, watching cars drive by on Appleton Avenue below. I was queen of the world up there. My cousins lived just west of us, on 89th Street, and they had their own neighborhood billboard. They packed sandwiches and ate lunch on their platform. But me, I just liked to sit. A billboard is a great place to dream.

When I became an adolescent, I often walked across the street to our vacant lot with my dog Corky. There, sitting on the warm weedy ground in the shadow of the scrubby trees, I confided all my troubles to her. One sultry summer evening, I left Corky behind and walked alone to the lot.

I was sitting on a big rock when the sky fell dark. I watched as the storm built. My dad had taught me how to tell how far away a storm is by counting seconds between seeing lightning and hearing thunder. I counted…five seconds, the storm was one mile away. Four seconds, three seconds…the storm grew closer. Finally, the lightning and thunder came together in a crash, and the sky opened. The wind howled and whipped my hair around. Rain pelted me. My house was right across the street, but instead of fleeing to it, I lay face-down on the earth.

That's me, "fishing" at a pond in Massachusetts near my grandparents' home.

I spread out my arms, as if in an embrace.

I felt safe.

I was home.

I HAD MY BOOK IDEA

Fifty years after my adventures in that vacant lot, I wanted to write a book about young people and nature. But where to start? Fiction? Nonfiction? A combination of the two? I shared my conundrum with a nature-loving friend, Mike Larson, who works at the Urban Ecology Center in Milwaukee.

"Why don't you come to Riverside and we'll walk around and talk about your ideas?" he asked.

Eventually I took Mike up on his offer. I met him at the Riverside Park branch of the UEC, where he and I ambled through the park's forest paths. He told me how neighbors and the Center transformed this place that had become home to drug deals and murder. He spoke about young people whose lives had been changed through their involvement there. As he talked, two things shone through his words: humor and compassion.

At the end of our walk, I had my book idea. No fiction, just the facts: it would be an account of how nature and the Urban Ecology Center changed the lives of young people. I only had to step aside and let them tell it.

RECORDING THE INTERVIEWS

In 2014 and 2016, I interviewed fifteen people ages fifteen through forty, using a tape recorder and/or taking hand-written notes. I wanted this book to be their words, not mine. Through all the interviews, I was struck again by what I felt when I first walked with Mike Larson at Riverside Park: humor and compassion.

I transcribed the interviews exactly. Later, I changed the order of a few paragraphs for clarity, and deleted some phrases because of repetition.

I took the whole year of 2015 off from the book project to sell a house, buy a house, pack and move from rural Menomonee Falls to the City of Milwaukee. During that transition year, some of the first interviews became "stale," so I offered each interviewee the opportunity to add a "PS" to update his or her account.

THEIR WORDS WOULD HAVE A HUGE IMPACT

"Wow, this is my city." That's what Shawn Office felt when he first canoed down the Milwaukee River and saw his hometown from a whole new angle.

Shawn is one of the young people I interviewed for this book. Little did he or any of the other interviewees realize, when they shared stories about urban nature encounters, that their words would have a huge impact on my life. Because of them, I realized that I could find my much-beloved nature right in the city. But my journey back to Milwaukee took a long and winding road... .

FROM THE CITY TO THE COUNTRY
AND BACK TO THE CITY

After falling in love with nature on that tiny vacant lot on the northwest side of Milwaukee, I became a nature nut. I sought nature wherever I went. In 1972, I married a like-minded man, Michael Sweet. In 1980, we bought an old farm house on ten acres in Menomonee Falls, located northwest of Milwaukee. The next year, we planned and constructed a solar retrofit addition to the home, and started our life in the country. We raised three children on those ten acres.

Our mini-farm became home to chickens, ducks, horses, and goats. We let our woods go wild and over the decades we watched new trees slowly "march" down the moraine at the end of our land. We let our prairie go wild and were surprised when a huge stand of blue bottle gentians established itself and spread larger each year. We couldn't see our neighbors'

Before Mike and I moved back to the city ...
our Menomonee Falls land at dusk

houses, but we often spied wild turkeys and white-tailed deer. We heard a peeper frog chorus chirp through every spring and coyote packs yip through every thunderstorm.

By 2015, we had lived there for thirty-four years and our kids had grown up and moved away. Every trip to visit them meant a long drive to Milwaukee or Franklin, a southern suburb. We were caring for more house and more land than we needed. It was time to downsize and move closer to our children and grandchildren and the places in Milwaukee where we go to have fun.

It wasn't only the interviews that influenced us to return to the city...but they helped. Between listening to the those I interviewed for this book, and wandering around each branch of the Urban Ecology Center, I realized that Milwaukee has

The bottle gentians that appeared as if by magic on our Menomonee Falls land

plenty of nature. If Mike and I looked hard enough, I knew we'd find a city dwelling with room to breathe.

THE HUNT

During our house hunt, my husband and I haunted parks and parkways. There are an amazing 15,000 acres of parkland in Milwaukee County, including more than 140 parks and parkways, many in Milwaukee proper—the "necklace of green" envisioned by the father of the Milwaukee County Park System, Charles B. Whitnall.

In September 2015, we purchased a house on Jackson Park Drive, on Milwaukee's South Side. We now live within spitting distance from our next-door neighbors, yet we have an expansive vista of the wild Kinnickinnic Parkway right off our backyard. Within the first week living there, I spied three familiar-looking creatures skulking about: a coyote, a raccoon, and a possum.

NARY A HOUSE IN SIGHT

At this writing, we have lived in Milwaukee for a year. Every morning, we cross the street and walk our dog along the Kinnickinnic River, on paths that I swear have been around since early Native American tribes settled the area. While we walk, we are surrounded by foliage with nary a house in sight.

One day on that river-edge path, I encountered a young man who was preparing for an adventure with a couple of friends. The young man held a grappling hook and told me he was planning to climb the giant rocks along the river. He announced, "I'm an urban rock climber. And sometimes a tree climber, too." He had also found nature in the city.

The Kinnickinnic River in the parkway across from
our Milwaukee home

Besides hosting urban rock climbers and tree-climbers, Jackson Parkway appears to be a popular flyway. We see more birds at our feeder than we saw out in the country—five rose-breasted grosbeaks at one time this spring.

My husband, who didn't want to move away from Menomonee Falls at first, is overjoyed to be living a mile from where he grew up on Milwaukee's South Side. He remembers summer times when he biked along Jackson Parkway and played baseball in the diamonds that were set up there, only returning home for lunch and supper. On one of our morning walks, he and I discovered one 1950s backstop still intact, overgrown now with vines and bushes.

Our memories are like that, overgrown now with ghostly images: children playing ball from morning till night along an urban river parkway...dancing "The Twist" on road-building equipment...and dreaming on billboard platforms.... .

We also have more than three decades of memories of living "out in the country." We will always love rural living and the little farm we made our own. But we don't miss it.

This is our city.

We are home.

August 2016

PEOPLE YOU WILL MEET IN THESE STORIES: WHO ARE THEY?

As the stories unfold, you'll find that the young storytellers formed their connection to nature as much through other people as through nature itself. Over and over, interviewees refer to Urban Ecology Center staff people by name. Here is a directory of workers who influenced the lives of the storytellers in this book:

- John Coleman IV, former weekend educator
- Beth Fetterley, now Beth Heller, senior director of education and strategic planning
- Dan Gray, former urban adventures coordinator
- Willie Karidis, former Washington Park branch manager
- Ken Leinbach, executive director of the Urban Ecology Center
- Kirsten Maier, environmental educator
- Jim McGinity, former research liaison
- Darrell Smith, former community program coordinator
- Rachel Soika, former environmental educator
- Robin Squier, citizen science volunteer
- Scott Stromberger, former community program educator
- Tim Vargo, manager of research and citizen science
- Susan Winans, former volunteer program coordinator

THE URBAN ECOLOGY CENTER BRANCH LOCATIONS

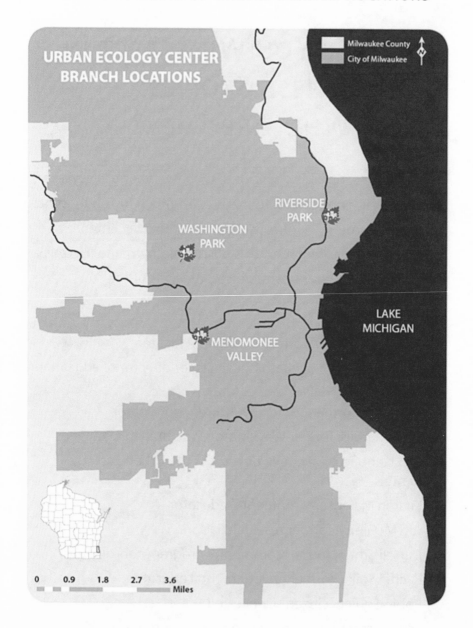

THE URBAN ECOLOGY CENTER
MISSION STATEMENT

The Urban Ecology Center fosters ecological understanding as inspiration for change, neighborhood by neighborhood.

OUR ENVIRONMENTAL COMMUNITY CENTERS:

- Provide outdoor science education for urban youth.
- Protect and use public natural areas, making them safe, accessible and vibrant.
- Preserve and enhance these natural areas and their surrounding waters.
- Promote community by offering resources that support learning, volunteerism, stewardship, recreation and camaraderie.
- Practice and model environmentally responsible behaviors.

Building and grounds at Urban Ecology Center Riverside Park
(Photo courtesy of Sarina Counard-Ryals)

"Although we did not set out to become a crime-fighting agency, one of the ancillary benefits of having an Urban Ecology Center in a park is that all the activity surrounding a Center tends to drive away crime. Since one of our goals is to give nearby residents easy access to nature, removing crime makes that easier. For those reasons, we seek out high-crime areas for our work."
– Ken Leinbach
Urban Ecology: A Natural Way to Transform Kids, Parks, Cities, and the World

THE STORIES

PART 1

RIVERSIDE PARK TEENS

Shawn Office, 23 years old at time of interview
(Photo courtesy of Shawn Office)

SHAWN OFFICE:
"I FELT REALLY RICH."

"I WAS ANGRY AND VIOLENT."

I grew up really, really poor. The majority of people in my family are really not educated. I was the first and the only to go to college. I didn't have that many options.

I always had a love for animals. I had dogs and I'd always catch random things in the neighborhood and I'd take them home and my mom would say no. But I never really thought about it as a "nature thing," as being larger than cats and dogs and random animals in the neighborhood. So, I guess I had a love of nature, I just didn't know there was more to it.

When I was eleven, twelve, thirteen, I kept telling myself I would be a cop, just to try to avoid the nonsense that I saw my family was going through, you know, like cousins who were in jail and doing stupid stuff. "I'm not going to do that, I'm not going to do that."

I went through a point when I was really angry and I was violent. You know, I was upset at my situation. I lived pretty close to the east side, on North Avenue and Palmer, which is sort of Brewers Hill but not really—the poor side of Brewers Hill. A few blocks down and it would have been gravy.

I was upset. I was pretty violent to my siblings. I wouldn't hit adults but I would be really verbally awful with people. I wasn't mean to my mom—I knew better. It wasn't like I wasn't being punished for the stupid stuff I was doing. Looking back at it, I didn't have an outlet, so obviously, it's going to be a re-occurring sort of thing…like okay, I'm going to get my behind whupped for this, but I don't care, I'm going to do something, I need to get this anger out.

I'd spend my days running amok with the neighborhood rascals. We'd go around and do stupid stuff. I was a skateboard-er at that time and we'd go to the Four Seasons skate park, but when that wasn't open, we'd do graffiti and stupid stuff.

There was nothing to do. Unless you had money, there wasn't much to do with the exception of going to places that are free, which is the Urban Ecology Center. But I hadn't found out about UEC yet.

Do we have to pay to be here?

My cousin Roger (page 46), he was hanging out with my little brother one day and he tried to get him to go to this place called the Urban Ecology Center and my little brother was like, "I don't want to go there." I guess he had been there before and he wasn't diggin' it.

I asked him, "What's that?"

My cousin said, "Just come on, we'll ride bikes and we'll hang out." There was some weird detail he described to me, I think it was kayaking.

And I said, "What are you talking about?"

"Just come, just come."

So, we walked into Riverside Park to get to the UEC, and this has to be pretty close to right after they had finished the building. They were still in the trailer a year or so before. The building is beautiful, beautiful. And we walk in and there's so much going on.

I asked him, "Do we have to pay to be here?"

Tim Vargo, he's in charge of research for the Center, and he walks up. "Hey, Roger, who's this?"

"This is my cousin Shawn."

"Shawn, how are you?" and I think he invited Roger on a bird banding, and I didn't know at the time what that was; I thought it was some weird dance or something. But he invited Roger to that, and then he said, "Oh! If you have time, you know, feel free to come along anytime."

Roger is a year younger than me, so he would have been thirteen. I was fourteen, getting ready to start high school the next year.

So, I'm in this beautiful building, which was completely weird. All I thought was, "This should cost money." You know, when you're approaching the building from the west side, the first thing you see once you walk into it is the animal room. I realized, *Oh, it's like a mini-zoo and there are animals every-where.* There's obviously tons of foliage and vegetation all around the center, and I kept thinking, *What is this place?* We walked in there when were done talking to Tim, and Roger walks me around the animal room. Roger knows every single one of these animals' names. He had definitely grown up in the center.

And he went ahead telling me about all these animals and I asked, "Dude, where do they get all this stuff?"

And he said, "All these animals are from here, they're natives of Wisconsin."

I thought myself to be pretty intelligent at the time, and I thought, *Dude, my little cousin is destroying me right now.* The male ego thing was totally going on there.

That day, I'm pretty sure we spent the entire day there, from early morning, right around the time they opened up, until about 7:00 o'clock. We had to run home and beat the street lights, or else that was your butt. Yeah, we spent the entire day there, I listened to Roger talk about this place. And I think he invited me back the next day and we hung out there again, but they had some event going on, and that was kayaking. I'm pretty sure that was my first time kayaking.

And then I got hooked and I would be at the center every single day. From my house, Riverside was about three to four miles the way we walked. We walked every day and spent all day learning something new. There were times they had guests there speaking about the Urban Ecology Center or nature—they would go out and they would tag snakes, we were invited to do that—all kinds of University of Wisconsin-Milwaukee research.

I think it was Beth Fetterley, who when I met her, I think on my second day there, I asked her, "Does it cost money to be here?" I didn't believe my cousin that it doesn't cost money, I thought they'd give me a bill.

Then Beth goes, "Don't worry about it. Hang out here anytime." And she basically went ahead and gave me a membership, just told me my mom had to sign a waiver.

They didn't have the rock climbing wall till later. There was canoeing, kayaking. They had a few bikes there that were donated from Dick Burke, who owned Trek Bikes—the largest donor to the UEC. All kinds of hikes, bird banding, they would do camping trips.

WOW, THIS IS IN MY CITY!

There was a group of the staff who invited Roger and me to go canoeing. We were walking from the UEC, helping to carry kayaks down to the launching point, and I've always been a beefy kid so I've never had a problem lifting. We were walking, and Tim was giving us a once-over of the park and pointing out birds and all this information, and I was super-impressed, you know, I'd never looked at trees like that or looked at nature like that.

Every few steps he kept pointing something out. I think Beth was there also, and there would be a cricket or something that would go off and Beth's degree relates to bugs somehow, and she'd say, "Oh yeah, that's this kind." She'd give the scientific name – *how can they have all this random information, this random knowledge?* – all the way down to the launch pad, and then again once we'd gotten into the Milwaukee River.

For this canoe trip, they'd paired me up with one of the staff members, I think it was Dan Gray, the former adventure coordinator. We were all as a group, and we went down toward North Avenue, and that's a decent little stretch for a first-timer. I had never seen the city from this point before because you're just totally surrounded by nature, you don't really see the road, you see nothing but nature, and it's totally compelling to a kid, you're thinking, *Wow, I never knew there was this much to do here.*

And this isn't costing me anything. I was really freaked out by it. You know, I'm used to the concept of paying for things. I knew I was poor. But I felt really rich.

I thought, *Wow, there are probably a lot of people with plenty of money who have never seen this.* It was very enriching, very fulfilling. I thought, *Wow, this is in my city.* I had seen the city but I'd never seen that part of the city, I'd never seen it like that. What was really weird about that situation, I think there were a bunch of salmon flapping around. It was around salmon run time. I was freaked out by it. I had seen people fishing in Washington Park—it was really run down at the time, the water was horrible, and there was carp and stuff in it. But I had never seen salmon.

It was like, "Wow, where did this fish come from?" all over the place. And frogs and all this stuff. Birds, snakes, and fish, oh my.

The Urban Ecology Center is really a strange place because they would challenge you. It would never be a day with you just screwing around. They would test all their little thesis points on you. "Hey, Shawn, remember when we walked in the park the other day, what was that bird I told you about?" Tim was like that and Beth was like that, they'd always challenge you. But I think because of that—and I think I was seeking that, I needed that, I needed that structure—I got hooked. I think it only took about a week, honestly.

I BECAME REALLY POSSESSIVE OF THIS PARK

I became a volunteer immediately. I was a park ranger; that was the first task I was given. A park ranger goes through the park and picks up trash, moves logs out of the way of the path, and it was rewarding to me at the time. It was housekeeping, but for this giant area. Like you walk through the park, you find little bits and pieces of trash, and I wanted to preserve this; it was beautiful. It wasn't like anything that I had had growing up, you know.

And I would get really mad at people, like "Who the heck threw this gum wrapper down?" I'd get ticked off about it. I became really possessive of this park, so I was constantly going through and trying to make it beautiful for people to walk through and see the same things that I had seen and become attached to.

WHAT WAS MY ALTERNATIVE? TO BE ANGRY AGAIN

I was a park ranger the rest of that first summer. I never missed a day. What was my alternative? To be angry again. There's no point in that. I'm just going to go around these pleasant people, learn something today. I didn't pack a lunch. There was always food there. It was a random thing. They would always get bakery stuff from Alterra, and obviously, the Center hosted a lot of events and people didn't take the food with them; they left it behind in that industrial-sized fridge in the basement. And they said, "Yeah, feel free."

I'd stay all day helping out doing whatever they needed. If it rained, we'd still go there. We'd be doing the park ranger thing or we'd be inside doing things. It was still fun. We'd hear different noises, see different birds willing to fly in the rain, you know, all kinds of weird stuff. It was much easier to see snakes that way because they'd lay boards down. In summer, the heat from the sun kind of super-charges these plywood boards, and the snakes want that heat, and they go under, and you lift them up and it's like, "Oh, look." We were supposed to tag the snakes.

THEY FLING THIS MUSK AT YOU AND IT'S THE WORST

To tag snakes, you take a piece of scale off from the snake from a certain point to where it grows back a certain way. You figure out whether it's male or female with some weird pin-type tool that I wasn't willing to do—like, "I'm not going to poke this snake's skin." They're really good at figuring out the age of the snake. The research department at UWM would come over and we'd work with them, Roger and I. They'd invite us over.

When you've tagged a snake, it tells you that you've caught that particular snake before, and where. Based on where you tagged it, you figure out whether or not you caught this, if it's male or female.

Butler's garter snakes can be small, but they can get to a decent size. When you reach down and grab them, they fling this musk at you and it's the worst-smelling stuff. When they originally launched that project, and I felt privileged to be a part of it, the Butler's garter snake was a threatened species at the time, and luckily, through the Center's hard work, it's not threatened in the park.

I BET YOU CAN'T

After I got involved with the UEC, my mother noticed a lack of anger in me and a huge improvement. I'd be exhausted when I got home.

Once school started, I went to the Center every day after school. I was also on the school swim team. I was a diver; I loved it. I brought people to the UEC constantly, girls and boys. I wanted to bring everyone. A few became volunteers later on in high school; a few became outdoor leaders, got jobs and internships.

I volunteered during freshman year. Then the following year, in tenth grade, I was invited to become an outdoor leader. Roger and I applied and interviewed. We could explain the park and assist with animal feeding. I got the job during the summer of 2007; it was a paying job.

I spent the first half of that summer working on environmentally-based summer camps around the neighborhoods. Along with other high school leaders and college interns and educational staff, I worked with people from all over, ages five through thirteen, from all economic levels. We went on hikes, bike rides, canoe rides, rock climbing. I was trained to be a belayer.

There was one little girl I'll never forget, who always liked to show me she was learning the information.

One day I met a boy who was like how I used to be. I was off work that day, hanging out at the Center, when a boy refused to come off the bus. It was a liability issue. They were supposed to get into the UEC's Prius and go to the lakefront. But the boy stayed on the bus and refused to go to the lake. Jonathan Kid said, "Shawn, please go talk to him." It was like, "Shawn, it's awesome you showed up."

I was one of those kids, like the boy on the bus. The kid said, "I don't want to do this stupid stuff."

I said, "You can hang with me."

The boy became attached to me. I coerced him into the lake. We caught catfish with nets and poles. With kids like that, you have to challenge them, you have to say "I bet you can't." By the end of the day, the boy was running around and having fun.

IT WAS ON FIRE

The second half of summer before my sophomore year in high school, I went to Teton Scientific School in Wyoming, in the mountains. It was a wake-up call. We used port-a-potties, had no showers for a week. We camped in tents for the entire week. We had amazing meals prepared for us—tacos and other stuff.

The purpose was to further our knowledge of nature. We assisted in surveys of the number of trees around the school.

Roger was there with me. Most of the time in the Tetons, we were tenting or hiking. We went to Cheyenne and learned some important points of American history, about the railroad and so on. We went to Yellowstone National Park and saw Old Faithful. I had never left Milwaukee before, had never been in a plane. It really worked for me.

On that trip, we also saw the scary side of nature. When we pulled up to our campsite, lightning had hit a tree and the tree was on fire. I had to be forced to get out of the van.

I STILL DO THINGS IN NATURE

I was a summer intern after sophomore year; that rolled into my junior year. I worked with smaller kids up to middle school age kids. I had taken over the animal room at that point.

I was influenced by the UEC to go to college. I once joked to Ken Leinbach that I wanted to take over the Center. He said, "You need to go to college." But I couldn't stand school.

I worked senior year and after high school at Green Business Concepts, a local recycling company. I had moved out on my own when I was eighteen. At Green Business Concepts, I started off dismantling stuff and then after three months, I was executive assistant to the owner. I was always a confident person, but now I had knowledge to back up the confidence.

I stayed at Green Business Concepts for three years. We became the electronics recycler for Shorewood. We'd host events at the Urban Ecology Center, where people could drop off their computers and electronics. The recycling was done locally; that's how we got the Center's backing.

Eventually, I was in charge of the customer relations management database. I kept emails, sent out emails about our electronic scrap.

I went to college at Milwaukee Area Technical College for environmental health and water quality technology. After a year and a half, I got bored. I never liked the structure of how you learn in school.

I became detached from the UEC at this point. I worked at US Bank, then for Mosaic Sales Solutions, and after that, for Samsung. It kept me pretty busy. I was twenty-two at the time; it was break time. I took a month off to travel to Mexico. I went on a zip line.

Then I got into the airline industry—first a brief stint with Frontier Airlines, then in March 2014, with United. I work in operations and do everything—customer service, marshaling airplanes, anything they need me to do. In Milwaukee, all the airlines have people multitasking.

I live on the South Side of Milwaukee now. I would absolutely work in a nature job. I think it was last year I interviewed with Beth Fetterley at the UEC Riverside location for an administrative assistant position. I would have loved to have gotten back to the Center. Someone else got the job who was way more qualified than I was. I breathe the Center but she was way more qualified for the position than I was, as far as analytic skills.

I still do things in nature. I'm a Freemason. Me and my lodge brothers go hiking. I was looking for the community like I felt at the Urban Ecology Center, and I found it with the Free-masons. We do fundraisers for the UEC.

IT'S NOT JUST YOU THAT'S SPECIAL

The Urban Ecology Center is doing a fantastic job paving the way for people of low economic standing to move up in the world. Sports and entertainment are the usual gateways. There are few African Americans in the sciences. The UEC gets people started with science education.

I believe that if people would become scientifically literate, that would solve the world's issues. Look at any issue in the world. If people were scientifically literate, those problems would be solved—like climate change, the war in the Middle East, unfair treatment of women in the workplace—it's because people are uninformed, thinking that other people are less than they are.

My wish for the world is that people would love nature and respect it, that people would be scientifically literate. That would lead to a greater appreciation for everything else. When you're scientifically literate, you realize that it's not just you that's special.

Roger Coleman, 23 years old at time of interview
(Photo courtesy of Roger Coleman)

"Of the teachers surveyed, 97% told us that their students had learned and performed better in school after their visits to the center.... We have had a nearly 95% retention rate in our school program since its inception in 1999. "
—Ken Leinbach
Urban Ecology: A Natural Way to Transform
Kids, Parks, Cities, and the World

Roger Coleman:
"You wonder 'What if...?'"

Things an inner-city kid would only see on TV

My typical summer day when I was about nine years old would be to wake up, fix a bowl of cereal, scan through TV channels to find cartoons or something interesting to watch, probably play a ton of video games. After, I'd usually head outside and play. I lived in the Riverwest neighborhood, which made it easy to play at Gordon Park or climb trees in the woods with friends. We'd do lots of things together, like playing at each other's houses and taking bike rides to Hubbard Park on the Oak Leaf bike trail.

In 2001, my mother took me to a Winterfest that was going on at the infamous Urban Ecology Center's double-wide trailer at Riverside Park. There was a lot of crazy, fun, exciting things that an inner-city kid would only see on TV: rock climbing, ice sculptures, igloos made of ice, winter bowling, sledding, and animals—like snapping turtles, frogs, snakes, and salamanders. I think my mom heard about Winterfest from a banner on the street, the Riverwest newspaper or an Urban Ecology Center newsletter.

I thought that every day was going to be like Winterfest, so I came back to the Center the next Saturday. It looked pretty desolate. I remember asking, "Where's all the stuff?" John Coleman, an employee at the time, offered to let me help feed the animals. This was the first time I actually fed them.

Me in a butterfly garden
(Photo courtesy of Roger Coleman)

I HAVE A BIRD!

I came every week to hang around on Saturday and Sunday. Then I started coming after school. The trailer was basically an animal room. The park had a huge spider web, a merry-go-round, swings, and much more. Eventually, I started getting involved with some of the programs they had, with a guy named Jim, then with Tim Vargo. We went on bird walks with binoculars, I then transitioned to bird banding and got to hold wild birds. I got to experience something you would only watch normally—to actually hold the bird. They are very fragile. I learned to be gentle. In spring, I'd either get to hold a yellow-bellied sapsucker or a cardinal. I went with Tim—there's actually a video of me at a bird banding site at the age of twelve or thirteen. I felt cautious, nervous, shocked, excited, dumbfounded: I remember thinking, *Oh, man, I have a bird!*

I introduced one of my good friends, Shawn Office (page 32), to the Urban Ecology Center, and he got very involved there.

GET CRACKING

I later headed to college at the University of Wisconsin-Platteville, and decided to go into Business Administration with emphasis on Business Management. I wanted to own my own business. I have plans for a clothing line and (or) a sophisticated jazz lounge, among a few other ideas. For school, I had to gain a three-credit internship, so I called the Urban Ecology Center… I did get an unpaid internship there.

The original plan was for me to be a volunteer outreach intern, where my job would be to create a volunteer recruitment plan. I did a lot of research, community outreach, recruitment plan work, and I also led volunteer orientations, tours and so much more.

After college, I wanted to take a little time off to have fun, so I applied to be a bartender. It's a fun, socially interactive job. At the time of searching for a good bartending gig, I was offered paid position at the UEC. I became an executive assistant to Beth Heller, the senior director of education and strategic planning. While working with Beth, I also kept at my volunteer outreach internship. These two positions added up to full-time. This is what brought me back to the Urban Ecology Center.

Most of my internship duties were indoor, but a big part of my job was community outreach. This was when I attended community events where like-minded organizations gathered to promote themselves. My job was to let them know we had a strong presence in Washington Park, and to also shed light on some of the great programs the Urban Ecology Center has to offer the public.

Nowadays, on a typical day of work, I usually come in to the Center and grab some tea, climb the tower, take in the scenery at the top of the tower, then get cracking. At the end of the day, I catch up with the high school teens who utilize our facilities after school. It's a good way to get to know them and for them to know that this is a really welcoming place to hang out.

I PICKED THE RED COLOR FOR THE BUILDING

There were a lot of transitions for me, from volunteer to summer camper to outdoor leader to summer intern to volunteer outreach intern to executive assistant. In that process, I have created a lot of wonderful memories. Some of my most memorable moments at the Center are the dripping ceilings in the double-wide trailer at Riverside Park, and having no running water. I remember putting up a giant spider web made of orange strings at Riverside on Earth Day years ago. I remember being on a backhoe to break ground for the building in Riverside Park. I picked the red color for that building. I

Me at the site before the Riverside Park building was constructed
(Photo courtesy of Roger Coleman)

remember creating trails in Riverside Park with a wheelbarrow and wood chips.

I remember a lot of personal adventures with the staff, like feeding the less fortunate with our executive director Ken's family at church and attending choir rehearsal with Beth Heller at her church. I have been to symphonies with a past employee, Darrell Smith, and even to Six Flags with Tim Vargo. The staff here are genuine and truly amazing.

YOU'RE SCARED AND YOU HAVE A CASE OF THE "WHAT IFS...?"

When I talk to other young people about the Center, I give my experiences from when I began to where I am now, opportunities like going to the Tetons and Yellowstone Park. I talk about taking a step outside my comfort zone. I think when you step outside your comfort zone, it opens you to so much you wouldn't have experienced otherwise. It creates potential newfound interests or hobbies, simply by trying something new. When you first go kayaking, canoeing, or hold an animal in your hand, you're scared and you have a case of the "What ifs?" – "What if it bites me?" "What if I drop it?" and so on. These experiences open doors for you. You become a lot more open-minded to newer experiences and learn things about yourself that you didn't know.

I don't know where I'd be without the Urban Ecology Center. I think there'd be a bigger chance of me being affected a lot more by the negative influences around me. In all those roles at the Center, where I had more than one job description, I found out I had the ability to do things that I didn't realize I could do.

Being active in nature can do a lot for young people. It can help them develop a conscious mindset of what it means to protect their natural environment and how important it is – it helps them develop an ecological understanding. You can become more sensitized to what's happening around you. You become more in tune with your naturalist side. You see a beautiful sight and stop to take it in rather than just continuing on your way. That changed mindset allows you to learn and teach what you know.

TAKE THEM

Kids like to be engaged in the learning process, so instead of telling them about nature, you can take them out and let them experience it for themselves. Take them to climb a tree and sneak in a few educational pieces about leaves, the use of sap. When you go fishing, you can look for bugs and talk about what you find. You can explain milkweed, how it's gooey inside— what insects eat milkweed to survive. You can find a caterpillar and talk about how it turns into this butterfly. These opportunities go on and on.

I'M BEYOND HAPPY

I want to continue on my journey of becoming a naturalist, day by day. I plan on continuing to learn how to be more resourceful and sustainable. I plan on soaking up as much knowledge as possible, and instilling that knowledge when given the opportunity to inspire youth, and open doors. I can't believe that I'm back at the Urban Ecology Center. I'm beyond happy. Not excited, more like I'm serene, at peace.

My dream for the Urban Ecology Center is not to get too big and lose focus on its main mission. My wish would probably be for the Center to continue to inspire youth to create a more knowledgeable and sustainable generation to preserve our planet's future.

My wish for the world would be for everyone to aspire to be open-minded to new experiences; that they would take the time to look, listen, and really feel the environment around them. If they did, they'd notice a lot of things out of place, a lot of things that could be, and a lot of things that should be left alone.

Painted turtle on a lily pad
(Photo courtesy of Matt Flower)

"In addition to the benefit of increased use of the parks, improved park safety, and investments, the ecology of each of the parks has been dramatically improved. Biodiversity has increased ten-fold, and the biodiversity of the acres converted to nature has increased in similar fashion."

—Ken Leinbach
Urban Ecology: A Natural Way to Transform
Kids, Parks, Cities, and the World

PART 2

RIVERSIDE PARK
CITIZEN SCIENTISTS
AND STAFF

Ethan Bott, 19 years old at time of interview
(Photo courtesy of Ethan Bott)

"I remember a survey in those early days that showed that fewer than 50 bikes passed by [in Riverside Park] on a warm, early fall Saturday. Two years ago, a similar survey measured bikers passing by in a day in the thousands."

—Ken Leinbach
Urban Ecology: A Natural Way to Transform Kids, Parks, Cities, and the World

Ethan Bott:
"The Wonders and Secrets of Nature"

THE SECRETS OF NATURE HAVE MADE ME WHO I AM

I have always wondered about things. That wondering has led me to do some wandering in the woods and on the water. What I found when I wandered was—wonderful! I guess you could say that the awesome wonders and secrets of nature have made me who I am.

As I was growing up, I was always the nature guy of the house. I have an older brother and sister, but I was the one who was interested in things like solar energy. I wondered how we could make our house more energy efficient.

IT DIDN'T WORK THAT GREAT,
BUT IT WAS FUN TO EXPERIMENT

My parents bought me a solar kit. I tried to create solar panels that would power a fan to cool me down, instead of using air conditioning. It didn't work that great, but it was fun to experiment. Then I thought about somehow making a treadmill in the gutters to produce enough energy to power a light bulb. I liked thinking about that stuff and playing around with it.

I wasn't always doing experiments. I ran around and played like crazy. I always liked hanging out with our animals—we have dogs and fish. My brother and I played football outside every day with the neighbors. Growing up in Whitefish Bay, I got to know a lot of kids through Little League and the Rec Department.

But even more than organized sports, I always liked nature itself. Maybe I take after my granddad, who was a zoologist. He knows a lot more about animals and nature than I do.

I GOT LEECHES STUCK TO MY LEGS. BLOODSUCKERS!

I suppose part of the reason I became a nature guy is that our family vacations were adventures outdoors. When I was really young, we went on cool road trips, like down the Mississippi River. We started in Minnesota, at Lake Itasca, the headwaters of the Mississippi. We went swimming, and I got leeches stuck to my legs. Bloodsuckers! I was freaked out.

We traveled all the way down the River Road and eventually we drove all the way back. There were many different natural areas to see along the way, plus the view of the river itself was always changing. We saw barges and houseboats. We were all amazed at the navigational locks on the river. I couldn't believe how the locks worked: they raise and lower the water so towboats and barges can travel past dams.

On another family vacation we went out West. I got to see deserts and mountains that look nothing like Wisconsin. The West looked more brown and felt more dry than the green rolling hills I'm used to.

When I got older, we started going to a cabin in northern Wisconsin, around the Spooner-Eagle River-Hayward area. We'd spend two weeks in the middle of August when my dad got off work. There was no running water, no electricity, no lights. There was a toilet that so slanted over that it was hard to sit on. We had to pour lime in it every time we used it to keep the smell down. We loved the place, but it was too small in the cabin for our family to sleep in, so we stayed in tents outside.

I COULDN'T BELIEVE HOW MANY STARS I COULD SEE
Lying in a tent there, I got to hear the animal sounds of the Northwoods night, where the traffic noise is distant. I couldn't believe how many stars I could see. The Milky Way is enormous, stretching across the sky. I never saw that many stars in White-fish Bay, where street lights and homes and businesses cast so much light.

That was our family vacation from when I was around ten years old until my mid-teens. Now that my brother and sister and I are in college and kind of going our separate ways, vacations are harder to plan. It was fun, though, back then, for all of us. We spent our time kayaking, biking, row-boating, fishing, and of course lighting camp fires.

I was the fire guy of the family. I always wanted to build fires even at our house in the city. We have a portable fire pit in the backyard in Whitefish Bay that I always wanted to light. My parents didn't want me to do it all the time. I guess it's not surprising that my love of fires led me to more wondering and ideas for experiments—I wanted to heat our house by fire. We have a fireplace but I don't think we had the right set-up to actually heat the whole house with a wood fire. It would have been great, though.

I COULDN'T TAKE MY EYES OFF THE GIANT SLIDE

A guy named Ken Leinbach lives down the block. He's a fun guy and he's friends with our whole family. One year, I saw him riding a huge unicycle in the Fourth of July parade. Afterwards, he came over and said hi to my family. He told us, "You should come and see the new Urban Ecology Center building."

My mom brought me there the next day. I couldn't take my eyes off the giant slide that starts outside and takes you inside. Over and over, I slid down and climbed up. That's my first memory of the Center.

The place became a second home to me as I was growing up. I was home-schooled, so my mom was also my teacher. I guess she saw the UEC as part of my education. She was the main one who got me involved there. One time she got an email from Ken Leinbach that said, "Hey, we need volunteers for bird banding." She knew I liked animals and being outside, and because of home-schooling, I had a flexible schedule. She told me about the bird-banding opportunity, and I said sure, I'd try it.

DO THEY PECK AT YOUR FINGERS? DO YOU BLEED?

When I signed up for bird banding, I wondered what it would be like. I mean—bird banding? Who does that? How do you catch the birds? How do you get them to sit still? Do they peck at your fingers? Do you bleed? And why would anyone do this in the first place? My head was full of questions.

They only do bird banding in spring and fall, and it was May-ish that I went for my first time. I turned thirteen on April 3, so I was old enough to volunteer. Most people at that age would be in school because bird banding starts at 5:00 in the morning and goes until noon or so. But because I was home-schooled, I was able to go.

I didn't like home-school in many ways, but it gave me this awesome opportunity. When I think about it, if I hadn't been home-schooled, I probably wouldn't have gotten as far as I did in my outdoors education at a young age. I'm glad my mom got all the information about volunteering at the UEC. I wouldn't have known how to find that on my own.

I LEARNED HOW TO REALLY OBSERVE

Once I signed up for bird banding, I went to a volunteer orientation with my dad. I met the volunteer coordinator, Susan Winans. She was cool and made me feel welcome and taught us the history of the park and importance of the UEC there. She's left the Center now, and is doing interesting nature things in Europe.

I instantly liked bird banding. Tim Vargo was the lead ornithologist/UEC guy there, and he was great. I loved it so much once I realized how much fun it was. I'd show up every Tuesday and Thursday at 5:00 or 6:00 am, riding my bike through the city. Once in a while, I got rides from my parents. I was the youngest person by far, by about thirty years. I enjoyed

I am holding a wild bird!
(Photo courtesy of Ethan Bott)

the people. I'd sit there and when a bird would come in, I'd help collect data. I learned how to really observe. It probably helped that I was a quiet kid. (I'm not so quiet now.)

THE BIRD LIES THERE IN ITS OWN
TANGLED LITTLE HAMMOCK

People sometimes ask me how bird banding works. We use a mist net. It's similar to volleyball net, but fine like those hairnets you see some people wear when they work with food. I think the mist nets cost a hundred or a couple of hundred dollars to make. They're easy to rip, very delicate. You have to be careful when you handle them. You set up two metal poles and string the net between them. The net goes down to the ground. When you look through the net, it looks like mist there. There are about four pockets in the net. When the bird hits the net, it falls into the pocket. The bird lies there its own tangled little hammock, soft and safe, until you come get it.

If it's really windy, birds can see the net and they avoid it. But otherwise, they're meandering on their way and they hit the net and poof, you've got them. We put out about eight nets every time and we have net checks every half hour. The people checking would be volunteers like me and Tim and also Jenn Callahan (page 88). When I first started bird banding, Jenn was a volunteer; she helped lead the project with Tim.

The first time we found a bird in the net, we were walking down the path and I could detect just a little movement in one of the net pockets. As we got closer, we could see yellow. Tim called it from a distance, and he was right: it was a yellow-throated warbler. He gently extracted the bird from the net pocket. He put it in a cloth bag, then carried it back up to the banding table. That was our headquarters at the top of the hill.

At the banding table, there were other volunteers, like Robin Squire, who was an amazing volunteer and knew a lot about birds. She slowly and carefully took the warbler out of the bag and began the bird banding process.

Now I'm stealing this example from Tim. Every time we had a banding project, he taught us that it's like a doctor's visit, what we do to the bird. When you go to the doctor's office, you get your height checked, your weight checked, your age and gender noted, and sometimes you get a wrist band that identifies you. We're doing this to get research on the birds because we don't know all that much about them. We test their blood to figure out their triglycerides, and we send the blood sample away to be assessed.

HOW DO THEY MANAGE TO GET TO THE SAME EXACT LOCATION?

It gets back to a kind of wondering about them, with a scientific method for finding the answers: How they know how to migrate? How do they manage to get to the same exact location every year? How do their young do the same migration? Is Riverside Park providing the necessary nutrition for the birds?

We know they're doing this migration for a reason. You could band year-round; that would be fine. But we're just really trying to get the birds that are passing through. I wouldn't want to be captured—it's stressful. But there's a reason for bird banding. When we keep records on migrating birds, we learn things that tell us what they need in their habitat. Then we can work on improving the habitat. With a healthy habitat, the birds will better be able to survive.

This is all part of what people are calling "citizen science." Land stewards are getting rid of invasive plant species, like buckthorn, which is especially bad for birds. The berries have low nutrition and make the birds poop fast, which only spreads the invasive further. We also try to get rid of invasives like garlic mustard and burdock. In UEC summer camp, we made buckthorn forts. There's some controversy about the term "citizen" in citizen science, as if people who aren't citizens aren't welcome. But in fact, everyone is welcome so a better term could be "community science."

Riverside Park is like a hotel for birds

I mean can you imagine being a small creature flying from Mexico trying to get to your breeding grounds? You need good food along the way. I sometimes think about that—the tiniest birds make such a long trip, from Mexico to Wisconsin. Riverside Park is like a hotel for birds. It reminds me of that long car trip my family took along the Mississippi River.

The birds are tired, looking for a good hotel. The birds travel over Lake Michigan, migrating during the night. They rise higher before dawn and when they run into a huge lake, it increases the concentration along the shore because they obviously can't land and find food in water.

I got hooked on bird banding from the first time I was part of it, and I've been doing it since then. At first, when I was young, I would just watch and see. In time, I went from watching to collecting data. Gradually, I learned how to teach other volunteers how to collect data. I learned how to check nets, then help take birds out of nets. Finally, I was actually able to hold the birds and take data on them. I still haven't done some things by myself, like really advanced things such as figuring out the age or sex of birds.

I could feel its little heart beating

Thanks to bird banding, if we catch a banded bird in Mexico or anywhere else, we can tell where and when it was caught before, and where it traveled from. We weigh the bird using a cardboard tube. I'll never forget the first time I got to do this by myself. It was tiny house wren, a secretive brown bird with a cocked tail. When I held the wren, I could feel its little heart beating against my fingers. For a second, I felt frozen. All I could do was stare at the bird—such a far traveler and so full of life. Eventually, after we took all the data on the bird, I was the one who got to let it fly away. It was an amazing feeling to do that.

I grew up with a bird in my hand. I kept doing it because I thought it was cool. I learned how to identify birds through bird banding. There are two types of grips: the bander's grip (gently holding down the wings to protect them) and the photographer's grip (putting two fingers under the bird's "knees"). You take the bird to your ear and listen to its heart. Hearing the sound of a bird that weighs less than a dime is truly an incredible feeling. So soft, yet so powerful and full of energy!

They've become like a second mom and dad

You need the master's permit to actually band birds—Jenn and Tim had that. Otherwise, we couldn't have done this. Jenn and Tim have been good friends for a long time. Through the Center, I got to know them well. They've become my two favorite people, like a second mom and dad to me.

I'd stay there until they closed and help them put things away. We'd have a table, donuts, coffee. I liked donuts at that age. They were a big treat because my parents wouldn't let me eat artificial coloring. Getting a jelly-filled donut was awesome.

I developed a relationship with Tim and Jenn and banding birds. After that, I got involved with all citizen science programs, like trapping for surveys—we trapped and surveyed turtles, mammals, monarch larvae, and snakes.

THEY'RE ALL FREAKING OUT

When I was in high school, I became an outdoor leader for the Urban Ecology Center. I worked in a new UEC program and loved it. I helped with summer camp biking adventures, going on bike rides, and I helped lead one trip from Riverside Park down to Lake Michigan on the bike path. The bikes belonged to the Center.

I bike all the time so I'm very comfortable on the bike and I never thought that other people would struggle riding bikes. These were sixth-, seventh-, and eighth-grade kids. I thought *Okay, they know how.* Maybe if they were younger, they'd have to learn to ride a bike. No, these were older kids. I thought, *Cool, a little biking adventure.*

We left and the kids were having trouble biking. I thought, *Holy cow, I've never thought of that.* I guess it was more of a deeper moment for me, realizing, discovering that wow, other kids don't know how to bike. I realized how privileged I was to be able to grow up with a bike. I remember teaching them about gears, how you can switch gears to make it easier or harder for you going up or down, and the kids were like, "What? That's so cool."

Bird in hand
(Photo courtesy of Ethan Bott)

They might have biked before, but not really. Some of them knew how to bike, but for a couple of them, it was totally vague and new. At one point, one kid who didn't use his brakes kind of ran into the railing when he came to a downhill part. We had stopped him before and said "Get ready." He kind of got ready, but not enough, so he ran into the railing. But he and the other kids loved biking once they mastered it.

In the same way it was cool to see kids discover biking, it's cool to go on the Milwaukee River with them, teaching them to canoe and paddle. Most kids have never canoed or kayaked— it's a learning experience for them—it's fun watching them learn. At first, they're all scared of the water, but by the end, they're comfortable being in the water kayaking and canoeing, which is really cool.

I always loved going to the animal room, either volunteering or working. Neal, the black rat snake, is my favorite snake. I remember seeing him first at the UEC and growing up with a snake always around there. I think his personality is really cool and great. I always pull him out for the kids. I love pulling out snakes because a lot of kids have never experienced or touched a snake and they're all freaking out. I show them how cool snakes are and explain how they're cold-blooded.

It's hard to describe snake personalities but I don't know, I guess I'd say that Neal would be chill and relaxed and calm and not going to bite. It's like with my dog. I have a strong sense of how he's feeling. I don't know, I have a kind of sense about animals. And I think other people know that, too, that the snake is relaxed and chill, so I always bring that one out.

HUMANS AREN'T FOOD

Snakes know that humans aren't food; we're huge, huge. Neal would bite only out of defense probably. I can't guarantee he's not going to bite you, but he's relaxed. He's been here most of the time I've been with the Center. I enjoy doing that at Washington Park now, too, pulling out the snake, letting kids touch him and feel and compare the bottom and the top of the snake, telling them how we catch snakes, why we do snake surveys. I find it really awesome.

Some kids freak out and leave the room. Others are freaking out but then they settle down and touch their first snake. So many of them never touched a snake before. Then I tell them "Hey, if you want to come out on a snake survey, you can catch a whole bunch of them at one time." They'll start screaming and saying "Oh, my gosh, that's crazy."

In Riverside Park, I think we have close to 5,000 snakes. There's a new Arboretum and they're trying to compare and contrast how putting in new plants and native species versus the old is affecting the whole forest. So, they're catching the snakes and tagging them, getting their weight, length, whether they're pregnant or not. They put diodes on them to see exactly where they go.

Some snakes travel quite a long way, like multiple miles—a little Butler garter snake can do that. There's a whole numbering system that we use. I think the number we caught over the entire history of the Center is about 4,700. The ones that we catch are brown snakes, Butler garter snakes, occasionally garter snakes. Those are native to Wisconsin. I don't think we've ever caught a black rat snake or a bull snake. They're natives, too. It would be pretty cool to catch one of those in the park.

People sometimes ask me why we care about snakes. I heard one example that helps explain it. Say you have an airplane and there are tons of little parts on it, and you can pick out one little piece of it. And you think, you don't know, you'll probably be safe. You pick out one little screw maybe on the window or on your seat. It probably won't affect you that much. But you don't know. And you keep picking out little things that will have an impact on the plane's safety. At what point are you going to say that's too many parts being taken out? In the same way, if we remove snakes because they are "scary," then we're constantly pulling pieces from the ecosystem, and at what time will that ecosystem collapse?

Snakes help control rodents. They're part of the cycle of the ecosystem. So, if you did take them out, it could have a larger unintended consequence on the ecosystem. They're a vital part, like any other organism of a natural ecosystem.

ONE HUNDRED MILKWEED PLANTS

This happened quite recently at Washington Park. We have something called the Young Scientists club—they meet almost every day. They went on a field trip on Saturday to fly kites at the lake. You have to be age seven to thirteen to go on the field trip. We had one young girl who was six, so she had to hang back with the other younger kids. I stayed with them.

I asked, "All right, boys and girls...you guys want to come on a monarch larvae survey with me?" I explained that what we do is count one hundred milkweed plants, looking for monarch eggs and caterpillars—they're called instars—and you look at every leaf.

I told the kids how the caterpillars will come out of the eggshell and become instars. There are five levels of instars. If you imagine first, second, third, fourth, fifth grade, at each grade level you look different. In first grade, you're small and puny. In second grade, you're a little bigger. By fifth grade, you're a big kid. So, I explained to the kids to think about monarch caterpillars in the same way. The first instar is teeny, pretty hard to see, with no color, just looks like a worm. Most people would say, "Ah, yuck, a bug." By the time it gets up to the fifth level, it's big, about an inch to an inch and a half long, thick and plump, with long antennas, yellow, green, black, beautiful colors. That's the fifth instar, which makes its chrysalis and emerges as a monarch butterfly to dry its wings.

When we do a monarch larvae survey, we're just looking for the instars and the eggs. The eggs are teeny, white, hard to describe. If you google monarch eggs, you'll see what I mean. The monarchs usually lay the eggs under the leaves. If you see monarchs hovering around, you'll probably find milkweed. They cling on it.

The little girl who was six years old and couldn't go on the field trip went looking for monarch larvae with me. Two guys came too, but they were way too distracted...this is quite an arduous process, turning every leaf of every plant over, especially when it's hot out. I told the kids about monarchs, their history, how it takes five generations to get from Mexico to Canada, and one super-generation to get back to Mexico to the one national park where most of them over-winter.

We started doing the survey and I was surprised—we found quite a few eggs at the beginning. It was really cool because the little girl was really amazed by it. "Oh, man, it's a monarch egg, I see monarchs, but I didn't know they laid eggs," she said. We kept going and we actually found an instar and honestly, when I do find them here, I'm surprised. I only found about four all last summer, so finding one that day was really cool.

We saw the egg and then the caterpillar. I wanted the little girl to count the plants with me. She did about two of them and

I did the other ninety-eight. It was a good sharing workload! She was only there for five minutes, but in that five minutes, we found a monarch on a plant just chilling out. I thought it had just emerged from a chrysalis. I told her it was probably drying its wings, getting ready to take flight for Mexico, part of the monarch migration.

She was all excited, talking to people on the path, "Come, come over here, look at this. Come look at this monarch butterfly." Then she left; she got bored. After an hour, I finished my survey, a really good survey. I came back into the building and I saw her again all chilling, and the other kids came back from the field trip.

The teacher asked her what she did and she said, "Oh we went on a... ." She had trouble remembering some of the terms so I had to help her out, but she was really excited and she told another staff member about what she did, really happy about the monarch that she found...she found it...especially after she couldn't go on the big-kid field trip.

WE ALL JOKE AROUND

The people who work at the Urban Ecology Center are awesome. We're all friends here, we all hang out, joke around, go for walks together. We get paid to work and learn, for example to learn bird calls. We're a real community. I believe that things are going to change for the better, through community. Something happens to you when you're part of one. It's like this: if I know you, I might work for change that would help solve your problem. If you know me, you might work for change that would help solve my problem.

After I started volunteering at age thirteen, I did more and more projects. I had a summer internship during my freshman summer. I was a high school outdoor leader, a paid position. I did everything: maintained the building, fed animals, did citizen science research, helped with camps. Of twenty outdoor leaders, they chose about eight to continue for the school year. I kept doing the same duties. From volunteering, I went to being an outdoor leader and finally to an adult internship. Glenna Holstein (page 204) did that and there are a lot of people who have gone through a whole series.

IT'S NOT LIKE A CANARY OR SOMETHING IN A CAGE

As I took on more responsibility at the Center, I got to see how things like bird banding affected people. I don't know if it changed them a lot; hopefully it did. Just seeing the thrill in their eyes when they held the bird and let it go, and remembering how I felt the first time—it's so cool. I mean, this is a wild bird; it's not like a canary or something in a cage.

It's like teaching someone how to bike. We're in the city— kids perceive nature much differently in the city from in the country. I live in the suburbs. A lot of the kids around here in Milwaukee don't have access to green space, so they live at home playing video games, board games, whatever, playing on the concrete, playing basketball. That's totally fine, that's their life, but I mean nature is where we came from.

Nature is our roots—it's us. I don't know how to explain it. It's important to be a part of nature, to be in it, to understand its beauty and power and significance and the amazing secrets it has. So, you take a kid through the park and we hear a bird and you use binoculars and find it. That's really cool. Finding monarch eggs on a milkweed plant, canoeing, showing them how to bike for the first time, or holding a bird—all these experiences are something that hopefully will affect them, make them appreciate nature.

ALL ABOUT A NEW WAY OF THINKING

I started leading monarch larvae surveys a few years ago. I used to find about eighty eggs in one survey; now it's hard to find ten or fifteen. I think it's caused by things like climate change, levels of ground-level ozone, or maybe it was the one year of terrible weather down in Mexico where all the monarchs winter.

Beth Heller and Ken Leinbach and Imani and I went to Tucson, Arizona for a "Systems Thinking" conference. It was all about a new way of thinking. Peter Senge is the author who coined the concept. It's about thinking of another person's perspective. For example, you can have three people going through the woods, like maybe an ornithologist, a land steward, and a mushroom guy. Each one has a different experience in the woods and observes and understands the woods. They're still trying this out at the UEC. Beth is going hard on that, trying to integrate it into the Center.

In Tucson, I also learned about "STELLA." It's a computer program where you can model population dynamics. You can study, say, a bird population and its deaths through loops and reinforcing loops. It was hard to understand, but interesting.

WITH COMMUNITY, YOU'VE GOT LESS CRIME

Through everything I've done with the UEC, my life has taken a definite nature direction. I don't know exactly what I'll do when I'm out of college. I'll be going into sophomore year at the University of Wisconsin–Stevens Point. Stevens Point has the best natural resource program in the state. I went in freshman year thinking one thing—wildlife ecology. I've always loved animals and thought this was the major to be in. However, after a couple of semesters, I realized this isn't what I wanted to do, so I switched my major to water resources. I wanted to do something with water because water is important and obviously vital to human life. Water in the world is not doing so hot right now.

So right now, I'm studying water resources which you could say is a little bit easier. It's more broad; hydrology is more specific. I wanted to stay broad and open. I mean when I apply for a job it's not going to be "Here, we have a hydrology job for you." So, I thought water resources would be a better idea. I could change; I have three years left in college.

It's hard to say exactly at this point exactly how the Urban Ecology Center has shaped me, because I'm still transitioning from childhood to adulthood. But I think it's helped in my transition to what I want to do. When I was younger, I knew I enjoyed nature. At the UEC, I had people providing me with the tools to succeed and grow in an environment where I would enjoy doing it. By being encouraged at the Center, I grew into wanting to do something with the environment and now at this point I'm pursuing a natural resources career.

I guess it's how I view nature and community. I think community is the biggest part. I've been thinking more and more that community is really vital. With community, you've got less crime. Everything comes from having community.

When I talk to young people about the UEC, I tell them it's a fun place to hang out. I tell them to start volunteering at thirteen and get involved. Really a lot of the main things have to do with whether you like animals, whether you like meeting people, helping out with programs, being involved with different cool camps. I'd encourage them to sign up for summer camp. I'd just say, "Hey, it's a cool place!" They don't understand that it's something more significant than another summer camp.

I love the Urban Ecology Center; they do great things. I'd love to be connected with the people forever, because they are awesome. I've been with the Center so long but I'm not tired of it; that's why I'm still here. But I want to see how different centers do different programs. I'd like to go outward too. I think Milwaukee's great, amazing, and I'd like to stay connected to the UEC, but I'd like to see other things too.

I hope the Center keeps doing what they're doing. I hope they'll continue to serve the community, provide the best they can, continue on their mission, keep protecting nature, and most importantly, connecting people to nature. I think as they are getting bigger and bigger and bigger, as more people recognize them, I hope they don't become such a big organization that they lose the sense of community within the workforce.

My wish for our world is this: I hope the world is a clean and safe environment—I know anyone else would say that – full of community, full of loving people who protect nature. I believe that climate change and global warming is happening and we don't have much time to act, and resources to stop it, so I hope people change their views and perspectives about nature to preserve and conserve it. Once we lose the earth, we're done.

PS AUGUST 2016 (21 YEARS OLD)

I am now majoring in hydrology with a minor in geographical information systems (GIF), and I have one year left.

I just got back from a backpacking trip in the Grand Tetons, a forty-mile route with elevation changes of up to two thousand feet per day. This place is incredible. It is so rugged and beautiful. We got to experience sights that most tourists don't see because we went backpacking into the back country so that we got an up close personal look at the Grand Teton itself. Talking about getting personal with nature, we had three bull moose tramp by literally next to our tent and stare at us just outside our camp…not to mention the elk, deer, trout, and other wildlife we saw.

It was amazing to be in the park on the National Parks Services Centennial birthday! The park service has done quite a lot, but the real credit and gratitude should go to the First Peoples, who were truly the first ones conserving these areas in the first place. My group had a great conversation on whether the Grand Tetons should be changed to the name that the Native Americans gave it or if it should stay the same that the

French named it. Being in these national parks gives me a sense of awe and wonderment. However, I want everyone to enjoy these areas. Too often the ones enjoying these areas are a majority of white people and I would love to see more diversity in these areas. If the national parks are a true representation of America, then there need to be other cultures represented in these parks.

I have changed and grown a lot since my freshmen year at college (at least I hope I have). I often reflect on what the Urban Ecology Center has done for me. Again, I think that the Center has changed Milwaukee by making green spaces a vibrant place for all people to enjoy and learn from. They excel at connecting and creating a community of bright-minded people. I hope they can continue to empower those around them. When people ask how can we change and make Milwaukee a better place, I know the Urban Ecology Center is a vital part of that process.

My last thought as I enter the workforce is about what can be done to create a more diverse place in environmental organizations, in the city, and in nature itself. Conservation has been done far too long by white men and I yearn for the day when other people and faces are a part of the movement. People like Sheldon Johnson, John Francis, and Rue Mapp are great examples and I hope they will continue to change conservation and what it means. I hope one day I can have an impact and know that I am welcoming to people of all color, gender, sexual orientation, etc. Without everyone on board, conservation is pointless. People are hurting, and the earth is hurting. Let's move on to create a loving world for generations and generations to come!

Konnie Her, 25 years old at time of interview
At Yellowstone Park
(Photo courtesy of Konnie Her)

"The head of the Department of City Development speaks nationally about Milwaukee's resurgence, and always includes two slides of the Urban Ecology Center in his PowerPoint presentations. He cites our work in job training for youth and in job creation, and calls us an organization that makes Milwaukee a more livable and lovable city, attracting people to live here and stay here."
—Ken Leinbach
Urban Ecology: A Natural Way to Transform
Kids, Parks, Cities, and the World

KONNIE HER:
"YOU'RE LIVING ON IT. DON'T YOU WANT TO TAKE CARE OF IT?"

OUT OF THE BUSHES SCURRIED A CHIPMUNK

I've always loved nature but was never immersed in it like I am now. It was like, "Oh birds, they're all the same. Plants, they're the same." My knowledge of nature was nowhere close to where it is today. Nor did I feel that I readily had access to the resources that I have now to be adventurous and explore new things. Growing up, my family did go on occasional camping trips, but outside of that we weren't very active in other recreational activities such as kayaking, fishing, or snowshoeing.

However, here is one camping trip that I'll remember forever...my mom decided to take my siblings and me for a hike while my dad stayed behind at the campsite. When we came back, we discovered him crouched down on the ground, staying very silent. He looked over to us and told us to be very quiet. Upon further inspection, I noticed he had parts of a Twinkie in his hand.

A few moments of silence went by, and at last, out of the bushes scurried a small chipmunk right into my dad's hand! I was so excited and amazed. He let all of us kids have a try and that is probably one of the first encounters with a wild animal that I can actually remember.

I also was part of a Girl Scout troop in elementary school and that is where I started experiencing new things. I was a tomboy growing up, always climbing trees and getting dirty. I loved catching bugs and "caring" for animals that didn't even need caring for. During my time with Girl Scouts, we went on many camping trips and hiked. We also went horseback riding and that was a first for me. I loved animals and nature and so at this young age, the only thing I could think of becoming was a veterinarian. As I grew up, that career didn't quite seem right to me. It wasn't until I was in college that I finally figured out what my true calling was.

Me at the Milwaukee Public Museum butterfly exhibit (2001) (Photo courtesy of Konnie Her)

"BIRDING? THAT'S FOR OLD PEOPLE."

I discovered the Urban Ecology Center during my junior year in college. I saw information about it online but didn't quite know what they were about.

I took a course at the University of Wisconsin-Milwaukee called "Breeding Birds of Wisconsin." It was the first year of the course, a collaboration with the Urban Ecology Center, and we were kind of guinea pigs. We were led by bird experts from the Center and from the Department of Natural Resources. It was the first time I met Jennifer Callaghan (page 88) —she was the bird expert from the UEC. It was a summer course that was one week long. We learned about birds that breed in Wisconsin; we traveled all over the state. This was my first time actually birdwatching and I felt overwhelmed learning how to identify birds by sight and sound. I was the youngest in the class; three were UWM students, including myself, and the rest were older adults who had come to the class through the UEC. There were fifteen total in the class.

We looked at color and body parts to identify birds like the yellow-rumped warbler. I felt really frustrated throughout the first few days...I could not remember the names of birds. Finally, on one of the last days, everything clicked. I started remembering birds. I felt so excited. Before that class, I thought "Birding? That's for old people." I thought it was crazy. I didn't think I was going to keep doing it even though I eventually thought it was cool. I didn't know I would go further.

I was majoring in biology but after that class and getting to know Jenn Callaghan, I changed my major to conservation and environmental science. I finally realized that what I really wanted to do for a career was to work outside in the field and to share my knowledge of the environment with others.

I got a job at Milwaukee County Parks as a land management technician. I did a lot of invasive species removal. There are a lot of invasives so there is "job security," as my boss would always say. I liked that job as it has taught me so much. I also did bird surveys. Birds are a good indicator of habitat health by seeing which species comes through. In a degraded area, you won't find many species—except for robins. Robins love buckthorn! In that job, we also surveyed salamanders, frogs, coyotes, crayfish, and snakes.

Me in the midst of invasive species removal in county parks (Photo courtesy of Konnie Her)

MICE AND NAIL POLISH

Prior to my position with the Parks, I volunteered at the Urban Ecology Center. I did small mammal trapping. Before that, I never had hands-on experience with wild animals for work experience. We trapped white-footed mice, some shrews and voles, occasionally a chipmunk. That year the UEC was building the Arboretum, and they wanted to see the mice population before and after its completion. Small mammals are one of the first indicators of where the environment is in its natural progression.

As part of our population study, we put nail polish on one ear. The polish would last two weeks and we'd get a general idea of how many mice there were in the area. We'd count them, look in their genital area to sex them, and age them by checking their size and color. I just loved touching the small mammals.

I DRAGGED MY SISTER TO DO ANIMAL TRAPPING

You need to find a balance between the world of technology and the natural world. There's so much out there that people are missing. If you are stressed out, you can go for a walk, get fresh air, and listen to the birds sing instead of playing video games or watching TV. I've influenced my fiancé to love nature. He now likes hiking. He knows that when we get married we'll do a lot of hiking, have a garden, maybe solar power, and aquaponics with fish.

When I talk to young people about the Urban Ecology Center, I tell them that the Center offers a wide variety of hands-on experiences. You can learn about plants if you don't want to touch animals. You can learn how to do research and data entry. You can go for recreation, like canoeing and rock climbing. There is something for everyone. I dragged my sister to the Center once to do mammal trapping and bird walks.

After my experience with the Urban Ecology Center, I spent two summers working with the Student Conservation Association in Milwaukee. It's all over North America, not just in Milwaukee. Despite its name, it's not solely based on nature; it's also about building skills for the workforce. It opens doors. I saw information about it on my school mailing list, applied and got the job. It was a paying job, part of a partnership with Milwaukee County Parks. We worked for six weeks in summer with at-risk youth roughly age fifteen through nineteen. There were two leaders for each crew of about twelve members.

The crews would remove invasive species and build and maintain trails. Every Friday we did environmental education. We as crew leaders made lesson plans, and we'd immerse them into nature; it was our goal to make them see nature in a new light.

You would see students on the very first day of the program not wanting to get their shoes dirty or touch a snake. By the end, they'd bloom and I'd want to cry. I always told them, "You've grown so much," but I'm not sure how seriously they actually took my words. Even though they were the ones who seemed to be changing, I felt like they changed my life as well. My mom was really proud. Just as I told my students, she said to me, "I've seen you grow and mature."

I think nature is a stress reliever. It brings the community together; people connect. "Weed Outs" at the County Parks is for volunteer work on certain days. I've been just blown away by how many people actually show up. On one occasion, there were about thirty people - Boy Scouts and surrounding community families all cutting buckthorn together.

I think nature also helps us appreciate the world and our environment. I mean you're living on it – don't you want to take care of it?

I WAS SO SCARED AT FIRST

I am moving to Minnesota. I will look for a nature job there, maybe something more mixed, involving education with children. Working with Milwaukee County Parks, I was sometimes given the opportunity to give presentations to kids and take them outside to explore the environment. Schools would partner with us to teach the students about birds or invasive species. I was so scared at first but it forced me to get comfortable giving presentations. I worked with a variety of ages at County Parks.

My wish for the Urban Ecology Center is that it can expand. Look at how long it took me to find it. I would like to see people recognize it more because it is such an amazing organization with a great sense of community. I hope to find something like it in Minnesota.

My hope for the world is that everyone would stop polluting and that everyone would take care of the earth. I wish that people would see its beauty. I feel if they would take time to enjoy it, and find what they enjoy about it, they would take care of it.

Jennifer Callaghan, 40 years old at time of interview
Standing in front of a rock formation at Joshua Tree National Park
(Photo courtesy of Jennifer Callaghan)

"As more and more people learned about us—at a conference, by word of mouth, or through the Internet—and the many impacts we were realizing in Milwaukee, they took notice. When they learned that the foundational activity of all of the impacts we were achieving had to do with simply getting kids outside and into nearby parks... well, they would sometimes laugh. It was so simple, yet also unexpected."

—Ken Leinbach
Urban Ecology: A Natural Way to Transform
Kids, Parks, Cities, and the World

JENNIFER CALLAGHAN: "IT'S A VERY SPIRITUAL EXPERIENCE FOR ME."

I RELATED SO MUCH MORE TO ANIMALS

I grew up in Florida, in the St. Petersburg area along the Gulf Coast. Nature was really important to me. My memories are filled with birthdays at parks, weekends at the beach, holidays camping and vacations traveling through the Appalachians.

My mom was very influential in my love of nature and how I grew to appreciate it as an adult. She enjoyed being outside, going on evening hikes, swimming in the pool, and playing card games on our picnic table in the backyard. Mom was responsible for getting us outdoors.

However, I think the biggest influence she had on me was through animals. She had an extraordinary admiration for wildlife and passed that to me. As a child, she and her brother raised an orphaned bat and kept it as a pet. Later, when my brother and I were children, she rehabilitated orphaned and sick wild animals before there were local organizations that did that kind of work. She rehabilitated birds and squirrels and even two "funny-looking, pink baby rats," which to everyone's surprise, later grew into two Southern flying squirrels. The flying squirrels were so young when she found them that they resembled pinky rats. My mother hates rats, but her compassion led her to save the little pinkies and raise them anyway. I think she figured they had a place in the natural world, too. Needless to say, she was incredibly happy to find that she was raising flying squirrels instead of fruit rats.

In fact, my brother and I had so many pets growing up that my friends lovingly referred to our house as "the zoo"—a wolf, snakes, ferrets, hamsters, turtles, dogs, and cats. I related so much more to animals than to humans. I was very shy as a child. I think I found it easier to understand their simple needs than those of the people I had a hard time communicating with.

Me with a baby squirrel
(Photo courtesy of Jennifer Callaghan)

WE RAN AWAY FROM THE ALLIGATOR

My mom's favorite story to tell is about a time when she was pushing my brother and me in a stroller at our favorite park, Boyd Hill Nature Preserve. There are gators and gopher tortoises there. Signs all through the park warn you about the alligators. As a family, we'd try to find the largest gator. They had taught us in preschool what to do if we ran into a large gator and needed to escape. And on this particular walk, we came upon an enormous gator on the trail, about fifteen feet long. My brother and I remembered what to do, and we did it. We jumped out of the stroller and ran in a zig-zagging fashion away from the alligator, leaving Mom behind to deal with it on her own.

My most formative nature memory, however, comes from an experience in late childhood. In my senior year of high school, there was an oil spill in the Gulf of Mexico that washed up on all of our local beaches. The images and thoughts of animals covered in crude oil were hard for me to stomach and I felt incredibly guilty that, as humans, we could cause such a catastrophe. My mom found an article in the newspaper about volunteers being needed to help with the oil-spill-cleanup efforts. One job that they needed help with was protecting the cages of the birds and animals that had been sickened or injured in the spill.

My family signed up for the midnight "raccoon patrol" position. The job entailed distracting the raccoons that were sneaking into the recovery enclosures eating or attacking the helpless animals. The recovery enclosures were temporary, shoddy cage-like structures, and predators could get into the cages easily. Volunteers were in charge of feeding the predators (which in this case were raccoons) in an area far from the enclosures so that the sick animals could peacefully recover.

Looking back on it now, I realize how short-sighted the solution was. I mean, what would happen to the raccoons once the humans weren't there to feed them anymore? Were we creating an unnatural reliance of the raccoons on humans? But in 1993, as I sat on the beach, under a dark, star-riddled sky, feeding wild creatures to help fix an unnecessary human-created disaster, I could think of nothing cooler. I contemplated a future in what I now know of as ecology. And I reveled in my first experience as a citizen scientist.

Me at a petting zoo
(Photo courtesy of Jennifer Callaghan)

JENNIFER CALLAGHAN

IT WAS SORT OF AN OUT-OF-BODY EXPERIENCE

I always intended to do something with animals; I liked wild animals. Then I was sidetracked by studying ballet. I got into ballet because I was born with a correctable leg deformity for which my pediatrician prescribed leg strengthening exercise such as gymnastics. However, our local gymnastics class was full and the employees at the local YWCA convinced my mom that ballet was almost the same as gymnastics. I took the class not knowing what I was getting into and later fell in love with the art form. I was a tomboy and loved the athleticism of it— the turns and the jumps and trying to do them better than the boys—that's what hooked me in the beginning.

My career as a professional ballet dancer led me around the United States, where I grew accustomed to a nomadic lifestyle. However, after dancing professionally for a decade, I tired of the politics of it and retired from dancing. For the first time in twenty-five years, I was unsure what to do with my life. I found myself lost in Milwaukee, trying to figure out what to do next. I needed some time to decompress.

I took long walks in nature with my little dog, Cricket. I knew I had always wanted to go back to school in preparation for a second career, so while I was dancing, I also went to college part-time. After retiring from ballet, I ended up at the University of Wisconsin–Milwaukee and chose biology as a major. Through biology classes there, I found the Urban Ecology Center.

I took a field biology class at the UWM field station about migratory bird banding. Through this class, I got to hold a wild bird in my hand for the first time, and it was a powerful moment. It was sort of an out-of-body experience: "This is what I want to do." I'm getting tears in my eyes just thinking about it.

So, I started volunteering at the UEC, many, many hours—like five hundred hours a year, heavy into research and monitoring. I finished my degree at UWM with a Bachelor's degree in conservation and environmental science and minors in biology and geography. It was very odd leaving my former life of dance; that had been a huge part of my life for probably twenty-five years. But I felt like I had found a real community at the Urban Ecology Center that was loving and accepting. I had found a new home.

TIM CONVINCED EVERYONE TO JUMP

I have seen a lot of people become involved with the Center. At first I worked there as a volunteer/intern for five years. After that, I worked as an employee for another five years. I was hired as the Research and Citizen Science Coordinator, which allows me to work outside in nature on research projects. All of our research projects have a volunteer component to them and we use community members to run some aspect of all of them.

Working with volunteers is probably one of my favorite parts of my job—I get to share wonderful experiences in nature with them and relive them over and over as if it's the first time. It is incredibly rewarding watching volunteers learn about our projects and become great citizen scientists. The coolest thing, though, is watching how closely connected to each other some of them become. They volunteer as citizen scientists because they enjoy the camaraderie and the togetherness. They often comment to me that learning about science is great, but the thing that keeps them engaged is the sense of community they find at the Urban Ecology Center.

When I first volunteered here, I was trying to immerse myself in the UEC culture. I took local eco-travel trips. Tim Vargo, who was then the research and citizen science coordinator at the Center, had a way of getting us into nature and enthused. I loved the people in these experiences and trips. One trip is burned into my brain. We were bird watching on the great sand dunes in Indiana with people from college age through retirees. At the end of the trip, Tim convinced everyone to jump off the top of a dune and had someone snap a photo of us all as we were jumping. Looking back, I can't believe he persuaded everyone to do this.

We all jumped off the dune
(Photo courtesy of Chad Thomack)

THE WHOLE BUILDING EMPTIED OUT

I recall another experience I had as a volunteer where I was surprised by the sense of family within the organization. I was participating in the turtle survey project, to get an idea of what species were in the Milwaukee River after the North Avenue dam was removed. We were using turtle hoop nets and captured an Eastern spiny soft-shell turtle that had a 22-inch carapace. We thought we may have had the state record size, so we radioed back to the Center to let staff know. The whole building emptied out. There were twelve people watching— staff, volunteers, facility guys. I was so shocked to see how interested everyone was in our project and how willing they were to check it out first hand.

There are a lot of high points like that for me now as a staff member. We have 20-plus projects going on in a field season. My favorite one of them is the odonate project (studying dragonflies and damselflies). These insects are largely under-surveyed and we started to survey them in 2013 when the Wisconsin Dragonfly Society asked us to start surveys in Milwaukee County. It seems their records had gaping holes since the year 1907. I had always had an interest in odonates; I remembered many dragonflies on our lawn back in Florida. But initially, it was a bit of a hard sell to our nature-loving citizen science volunteers. Then last year, the survey project took off. Our core group came again and again and got good at identifying. One man latched onto odonates because he couldn't band birds anymore due to a tremor.

Another favorite memory from the project was a time we were using a hand-lens to look at the jewel wings of the dragonflies. An artist was sketching in the group and she told her art class about it at Wisconsin Lutheran College. The art students came to watch one day but there were few dragonflies. Finally, we saw some on a hill at the Menomonee Valley UEC location. The students ran and caught the dragonflies; they couldn't get enough. The volunteer with the tremor was there, and it was his moment to shine. A dragonfly will not be hurt if it is held correctly. He held it while the art students sketched and produced beautiful color penciled representations of the jeweled creature and then let go of it as we all watched it fly away.

The small mammal monitoring project was fun too. We set live traps in the evening in the park, and check them in the morning. We collect data and mark the animal's ear with nail polish. The color we use matches the area or habitat in the park.

I WANTED TO BE CLOSE TO THOSE I WORKED WITH
My life has changed as a result of my being part of the UEC. I've got probably one of the only jobs in the state of this kind and I get to do what I love to do. There are few other organizations in Wisconsin that incorporate so much citizen science into their programming. When considering a second career, I knew I had to be out in nature and connect to it on a daily basis. It's a very spiritual, almost religious experience for me. If I didn't have the job, I would definitely still be a volunteer.

And the Urban Ecology Center gave me a second family. I didn't know I'd be able to find that "family" experience; I had that in dancing also. I wanted to be close to those I worked with.

The girls thought I was crazy

Nature can do a lot for people's lives. I recently met a young person who has a really hard home life. This person wanted to go on a bird walk "to feel free." We can have great spiritual/meditative moments in nature, and we can connect in a way that we don't usually connect anymore. When we go out into nature, we slow down. We observe things we don't typically observe, like feeling light on our skin or looking closely at a dragonfly wing. I want this for young people—a break in their eight-hour school day. Also, we see great benefit from science education and nature. I am proud to be a scientist and an educator.

One summer, I worked with two girls who met when I was co-teaching a UWM Birds of Wisconsin class. The girls really liked birding and they really liked the Urban Ecology Center. They found out about mammal monitoring and started volunteering with the project. Every time we'd catch a small mammal, the girls would say, "This is the coolest thing ever." I still get texts from those girls weekly. One of them told me, "I have you to thank for my double major in natural science and art." That is a rewarding thing to be told.

When I talk about the UEC, it depends on who I'm speaking to. If they like outdoor activities, I'll speak about the outdoor lending equipment program. If they're into animals, I'll tell them about the work I'm doing and recruit them to help. If they're into plants, I talk about our restoration land stewardship program. If they enjoy adventures, I tell them about eco-travel. There are many different avenues to come into the center. People most often tell me that what they like is that the people are so friendly at the UEC and the whole place is so community-driven.

If I wanted to talk to young people about nature, I wouldn't say anything, but I would let them experience something. Find an animal and watch it. How many faces I've seen transformed to see an animal up close in the wild! Maybe not a large snake, because of fear, but maybe a little tiny snake. The bird- banding project is a powerful tool, too. I like to let young people learn through their own experiences.

Once when I was teaching ballet in Illinois, a bird called outside the studio window. I said, "Oh, that's a chimney swift." The girls thought I was crazy. But one of the girls was intrigued, and she came up to Milwaukee to do bird banding with me, early in the morning. For a high schooler, 5:00 am is an adventure. She had a phenomenal experience. She had an excused absence from school to do the banding session. When she went back, she told her science teacher about her experience. He wanted to come out. It was great for me to expose my other students to nature this way.

I even got my stepdad to hold a wild bird when he stopped through Milwaukee once on a month-long motorcycle adventure from Florida to Alaska—it's one of his favorite stories to tell.

"HOLY COW, IT'S ANOTHER FOX!"

Last spring, I was leading a group of birders through the newly restored parcel of land in the Arboretum at Riverside. We were all a bit cranky because it was spring, but winter just wouldn't let go. The group was grumbling a bit walking through the new parcel because that section of the walk is typically the windiest and coldest part. We got to the section of the path on the hill that overlooks the river which was still completely frozen and covered with old snow.

We heard some noises on the west bank of the river that we assumed were dogs or noisy walkers because branches were cracking and moving around. Suddenly, a red fox comes barreling out of the woods and onto the ice. It was being chased by what we thought was a dog crashing around and breaking leafless branches in the way.

Then, the "dog" came bursting out of the bluff and onto the ice in pursuit of the fox, when we realized that "Holy cow, it's not a dog, it's another fox!" And so, the two of them chased each other back and forth down the river in front of us several times, and then took off around a bend in the river we couldn't see past.

It was one of the most phenomenal and surreal moments I've ever had in nature, like we all became frozen in time. I can still remember how unbelievably quiet the group became and how spellbound we were by the moment. The fact we were watching through our binoculars made the scene that much more real. We could see the fine details of the foxes' pelages and the beautiful, rusty-red color of their fur. Red foxes are really susceptible to sarcastic mange and it can actually shorten a fox's life, but these weren't your typical mangy urban foxes—they were shiny and healthy and completely unconcerned that a group of ten people was immersed in their wild fox lives in that moment. The group couldn't even speak for a good thirty seconds after the foxes disappeared because we were so caught up in the moment. I can still remember the face of the birder at my side as she stared wide-eyed after the scene unfolded.

But, the coolest thing is this: that sixty-second moment created a permanent change. That one sixty-second encounter changed how the birders felt about that cold and windy section of the walk. That part of the walk changed to a section that people anticipated and looked forward to instead of dreading.

A BALD EAGLE CLOSELY HOVERING

Since then, many cool sightings have happened on that hill. A coyote has been seen so many times on the hill that it has been dubbed internally as "Coyote Hill." Our birders spent the entire winter around the area, tracking a northern shrike that had moved in from the Arctic. Shrikes are fairly rare in Milwaukee and had never been documented in any of the Center's green spaces before.

Last summer, a co-worker witnessed a bald eagle closely hovering over that exact spot. It soared over her long enough to give her and her volunteers a detailed look, and then faded away farther into the sky. Many visitors have told us of spiritual-type encounters they have had in the new Arboretum area. We really treasure the space and I personally believe there is some kind of magical presence that often exists there.

MANY URBAN YOUTH LIVE BLOCKS FROM THE RIVER

I plan to keep involved with the Urban Ecology Center. Even if I didn't work here anymore, I would find a way to still be involved. One of my greatest wishes for the UEC is that it will bring nature to inner-city children on a larger scale. I can't believe how many urban youth live blocks from the river, but have not experienced it. I hope the Center can bring it to them.

With the political nature of our country, I'd wish that science and nature get the respect and the audience they deserve. We're not going to be able to deny it forever, that there are consequences of how we've neglected our world.

PS DATED AUGUST 2016

Since I gave this interview, my stepdad died from cancer, but until his last coherent day alive, he fondly remembered the Urban Ecology Center and his experience holding a wild bird. One of his "if I had it to do again" desires in life was to be a national park ranger. I think he enjoyed living vicariously through my work and imagining some of the beautiful things I am fortunate to experience daily.

Sunset at the UEC
(Photo courtesy of the Urban Ecology Center)

Julia Robson, 26 years old at time of interview
(Photo courtesy of Julia Robson)

" ... we were invited into a strategic planning process of the U.S. Forest Service called the Chief's Review. There we met with the top leadership of the 20,000-strong army of employees whose mission it is to steward our country's forest lands. We were there because the agency had realized the need for the urban populations in the U.S. to have more exposure to nature in order to develop awareness and caring about forest resources."

—Ken Leinbach
Urban Ecology: A Natural Way to Transform
Kids, Parks, Cities, and the World

JULIA ROBSON:
"IF WE MAKE LESS UNKNOWN, THERE WILL BE LESS FEAR OF THE UNKNOWN."

I REALIZED I COULD MAKE A DIFFERENCE

It's really hard for me to remember how I got close to nature; it feels innate to me. I asked my mom what fostered my deep connection with nature. I grew up in Miami. In third grade, we found some burrowing owls on top of a mound of sand. They would hide. Some children tried to kick in their nest. I told my mother. She went to the school board with me. We told people at the school about the owls. We went to the Humane Society and they gave us fencing to protect the owls.

It was one of the moments when I realized I could do something to make a difference. I saw different people working together. The principal wasn't fond of losing playground space to the owls, but agreed to help anyway. My mom always put us outside. We'd paint outside. We stayed in the yard because our neighborhood wasn't safe.

When we moved to Wisconsin, our neighborhood was safe and we could go outside and play for hours. We lived in Kenosha County near Silver Lake. That's where I found my first brown snake. We played in a two-acre wood lot that wasn't ours. I wrote a letter to Bear Realty almost begging them to leave the woods for the kids. They were so nice and wrote back.

HE LET ME SEE HIM AS IF HE KNEW ME FOR YEARS

My mom bought me a five-dollar *Birds of Wisconsin* book. I picked out a scarlet tanager and said, "I want to see this. How can we get to see this?" My mom bought different types of food and feeders. For seventeen years, I never saw a tanager. But one of the first days as Jacobus Park in Wauwatosa, while I was pulling up a sea of garlic mustard, not ten feet from me, a beautiful male tanager sat and sang. He let me see him as if he knew me for years. It was my best garlic-mustard-pulling day ever. After that incident, I became invested in birds. I'm an avid birder and I still have that ratty bird book.

In high school, I was running in a cross-country race in Sheridan Park just north of Warnimont Park. I noticed white cedars and goldenrods growing from the bluff and I could see downtown Milwaukee. I stopped. My coach was not happy with me. That was when I changed my mind about going to Stevens Point or Florida for college. I wanted to work with people and nature where they meet.

I'm so fascinated and passionate about the natural world. I completed my undergraduate degree in the Conservation and Environmental Sciences program at the University of Wisconsin–Milwaukee. I believe I would like to go back to school eventually, but I didn't want to go to graduate school right away because I always had a hard time knowing exactly what it was that I wanted to focus my studies on. For instance, restoration ecology? or population ecology?

IT DIDN'T EVEN HURT

Throughout college, I looked for volunteer work and internships I could do. I saw flyers. One was for an internship working with snakes. My mom was terrified of them. By applying for this internship, I could address my own uncomfortableness with snakes. It was through the University of Wisconsin–Milwaukee that I was hired as a site manager for a graduate student working on his project. I was afraid of being bitten, but I wanted to get it over with. The first time I was bitten by a Butler's garter snake, I didn't even notice it was happening. It simply felt like my skin was being rubbed with the rough side of Velcro. It didn't even hurt.

Me holding a Coho salmon in Oak Creek
(Photo courtesy of Julia Robson)

SHE HAD LITTLE LUMPS WITHIN HER BELLY

My fear of the unknown turned into a passion. During my internship, I told my mom, who lives in Kenosha, "Let's go to Milwaukee. We'll go shopping maybe." We went to my snake research site. I found a Butler's garter snake that was gravid, or pregnant. She had little lumps within her belly that I could feel, which were her eggs. "You're a mama," I said. My mom was suddenly connected. A Butler's garter snake has eggs that hatch on the inside of her body. She passes twelve to twenty young snakes to the outside of her body.

I've seen again and again that when people understand nature, it evolves into an appreciation. Now my mom is an advocate for snakes. She laughed about not shopping that day.

At times, it can be harder working with groups of people who are older. Younger people have minds that are very much open. Nature is a part of our lives whether we realize it or not. I don't have a lot of friends who are outdoorsy. But I've never met somebody who doesn't say "Neat" or "Cool" when we're outside together and I tell them something about a tree or bird or frog.

If they don't like nature or the outdoors, I try to give them something they will remember. They see my passion and they get excited even if they're uncomfortable at first about being in a wetland.

Once I was leading a group doing gray wolf tracking and there was a woman scared about bobcats. I told her about what they have to do going through hard conditions in winter. My passion made an effect. It's like when you have a professor or teacher who is engaging, you get interested.

It doesn't matter what walk of life you come from, nature is always available to you—you can enjoy it however you choose to. Sometimes I ask, "Do you like hiking?" If they say yes, I tell them, "Then you like nature. You get joy and relaxation from enjoying nature."

In school, when I was all stressed, I'd go on a hike. It relieved me to see all the interconnectedness. It relaxes me just to see this complex interwebbing, the beauty of plants and nature in an upland hardwood forest or a grass prairie. It's all so soothing. Nature just does this for people. Nature is the remedy to everyday stress, an escape.

THE NATURAL WORLD NEVER STOPS

Why do people walk? There's a reason. It brings you back to your roots. There's something about being way out in nature. The natural world never stops. It's always moving, buzzing, doing something. When you sit in the woods, you hear the birds singing. The wheel is always turning. It's awesome for five minutes or for the entire day.

WE MANAGE TEN THOUSAND ACRES

I feel excited to go to work every day. I'm the assistant natural areas coordinator for the Milwaukee County Parks Department. We manage ten thousand acres of natural areas within the county. It's an extensive land base for habitat management and restoration. I've been there five years; I started as an intern. We work to remove invasive species and re-establish natives. We also do wildlife monitoring—we see who is there before we work on the land.

Me holding a recently-banded female wood duck as part of a research project
(Photo courtesy of Julia Robson)

At first this was a "citizen science" program. We also worked with the Urban Ecology Center on snake monitoring and other things through their fantastic Citizen Science program. Before I worked for Parks, I worked for the Urban Ecology Center conducting their snake research.

Urban areas are often stereotyped as having little to no biodiversity. Through our work, we've disproved that. There are more than seven hundred species of plants. Over eighty percent of them are natives. We have observed over two hundred species of birds in the parks. We wanted to model a citizen science program after what the Urban Ecology Center does because people didn't realize what we have, even though the parks are in their backyard. There is so much biodiversity in county parks in spite of being so urban.

One of the most successful programs is our citizen-based wetland monitoring program. We provide training and equipment to families, students, and retirees. They monitor and collect data at four hundred and thirty ephemeral wetlands. There are only two full-time employees to manage the Parks Department's natural areas. We got a small grant from the Department of Natural Resources. We bought the equipment they use.

Parents and children are so excited monitoring the wetlands. They know they're contributing. The data helps us make management decisions that won't negatively impact organisms and will hopefully benefit them. For example, wood frogs in Milwaukee County: we want the critters to be here years from now. We must figure out how to conserve urban wildlife. There are sensitive natural systems amidst urban sprawl, and globally we're becoming more urban.

YOU CAN BE "GIRLY" AND GO OUT IN NATURE

One retiree I worked with lived in the city and she wanted to move to be in nature. She had no idea there were volunteer opportunities here in Milwaukee and frogs calling like they'd be up north. If you don't have a cabin up north, you can spend time in nature here in the city.

One of the citizen science groups that volunteers is the Franklin Ecology Club. We had the *Milwaukee Journal Sentinel* out with us to do a story on our partnership. The instructor and two girls were showing everyone how they check traps for crayfish. I saw a huge snapping turtle. I grabbed it. The color drained out of the girls' faces. The turtle looked so prehistoric. It was about fifteen inches across its shell. The teacher was laughing—the wetlands are not so "innocent" looking any-more.

I feel that you can be fabulous and "girly" and go out in nature. Just because I'm an outdoors woman doesn't mean I can't be "girly." I can have a manicure even with slimy hands. I'm the only girl in my family. My mom always put me in dresses even though I'd get all mucked up. I really do attribute my attitudes to her. She'd let us go out there and touch things, not just look at pictures in a book.

Me with a couple of snappers!
(Photo courtesy of Julia Robson)

"WILL WALKING ON LEAVES HURT ME?"

I don't expect everybody to have the passion for the natural world and do what I do, but I hope we get to the point that people understand and respect the world and organisms we share the world with. This comes from working with urban natural resources. I love "Up North" but the challenges we face because of people are one of the highlights of this field: we're showing people what's happening.

It comes down to respecting things. If you see a turtle in the road, you don't swerve to hit it. You maybe help it across. You don't throw garbage around, out of respect. You wouldn't go into a building and litter. It's the same idea.

Parents have the responsibility to decide if they want their children to have a relationship with nature, a connection that builds. Parents put limits on video games but sometimes provide little exposure to nature for their children. There is a bio-phobia in kids who don't get outside. One kid asked me, "Will walking on leaves hurt me?"

If we make less unknown, there will be less fear of the unknown.

Washington Park Urban Ecology Center building and grounds
(Photo courtesy of Sarina Counard-Ryals)

"I also shared that when we'd started in the 90s, going into the park alone was not a wise action to take, even for a grown man, but now a grandmother could take her young grandkids down to the river without even a thought about crime, thanks largely to all the positive activity that everyone on our team made happen each day."
—Ken Leinbach,
Urban Ecology: A Natural Way to Transform
Kids, Parks, Cities, and the World

PART 3

WASHINGTON PARK
YOUNG SCIENTISTS
AND STAFF

Katrina Young-Harris (39 years old at time of interview) speaking to donors and supporters at the 2014 UEC Summer Solstice Soiree, Riverside Park (Photo courtesy of Matthew Gnas)

"Some days we look at our list of impacts on all these different levels —from one kid or family in the neighborhood, to the impacts on the city, to the ripple effect that's taking the Center's vision out into the world—and feel like maybe we're onto something."
—Ken Leinbach,
Urban Ecology: A Natural Way to Transform Kids, Parks, Cities, and the World

KATRINA YOUNG-HARRIS: "HE SAID 'WASN'T NO BLACK KIDS ON NO FIELD TRIP WITH NO UEC.'"

I WAS DEPRESSED, LOCKED UP IN THE HOUSE

Before the Urban Ecology Center became a part of my life, it's easy to tell you what my world was like. A typical day for me was this: I was depressed, locked up in the house, hurt, afraid, scared. I didn't want to have anything to do with people.

Here's why. My house had got broken into while we were in it. I opened my eyes and saw the man standing over my bed, with my television in his hands. Also, my car got stolen. And I was just so disgusted. I was also going through things with my landlord and I was staying in a dump. I was very angry with the world, with people in general. I was mad.

STUFF I COULDN'T AFFORD IN
MY WILDEST DREAMS

I'm a single mother of three—my daughter is twenty-one, and I have Donald (page 128) and CJ, who are thirteen and fourteen. My boys loved me so much, they saw that I was in this deep depression. My house was dark—I didn't want any light in the house. I barricaded the doors and windows. They asked me to come out the house and go to the UEC with them.

My first outing with the Center was a field trip with my sons to Sheboygan at a science fair that some of the colleges were putting on. We were walking around, just observing different experiments. Some of them we could interact with. They blew up stuff. We walked on corn starch. I mean it was just something different and a nice way for me to get out. It woke up something in me, but even more so it was my kids caring so much about me to say, "Hey look, you can't continue this, locking yourself up in this house like this." It got me out. I think I had more fun than they did. They didn't want to be bothered with me once we got there; they left me by myself. I had such a good time.

My boys had been involved with the UEC since grade school and they were starting middle school at that time. They had been on a lot of field trips, they had went camping, stuff that I couldn't afford with my wildest dreams. The Center paid for everything, everything. And so, my way of giving back was becoming a volunteer. I always stressed further education with my boys, because I have an Associate's Degree and I can't find a job in my field. But they have to go to school, because I want them to be better than I am, to have more than I've gained. So, I talk about college to them all the time.

My oldest son, Donald, wants to be an ornithologist, a person who studies birds. Donald just had, about four or five months ago, a trip with all expenses paid, to Cornell University, the school that is at the top of his list for ornithology. Cornell sponsored a trip for him and another one of the Young Scientists from the Washington Park branch of the UEC. Donald was gone for a whole week, visiting their ornithology department.

I FINALLY WANTED TO DO SOMETHING TO MAKE THINGS BETTER

My boys have literally grown up in the eyes of the Center. They went on many, many trips. Willie at Washington Park told me that he was molding and shaping my boys to take over because he has to retire one day and he wants somebody to fill his shoes. My youngest son don't like the UEC as much as the oldest one. The oldest loves the Center, breathes it.

After I got involved with the Urban Ecology Center, I can tell you I could see a change in my life, period. It gave me a reason to get out and want to be around people again. I finally wanted to do something to make things better instead of complaining and crying about it.

THEY CAUGHT A MAN TRYING TO STEAL A CANOE

Instead of my sons getting in trouble and hanging out with the knuckleheads in the neighborhood, they have the UEC to go to. I had a blowing-out debate with one of the park workers one day.

I went to pick my sons up from a field trip. They got off late at Washington Park, and the park worker told me, "There wasn't no black kids on no field trip with no UEC."

I said, "I don't know what you talking about."

I trust people at the Center with my boys. I don't care where they take them, I know they're not going to hurt them, I know they're not going to harm them, I feel like they're in a safe place.

But me and this janitor had a blowing-out argument about urban kids don't like science.

And I'm like, "Are you serious? That's not the way you're supposed to talk to anyone; yes they do, and I'm going to show you because I'm going to make them get out of the car and wave at you when I pick them up."

And he was so shocked and surprised to see my boys there.

Since we all got involved with the Center, the boys are more open with me. We talk about almost everything, especially things about nature, like insects. If I see something and I don't know what it is, I'll ask them. They tell me – especially the bird thing. They know them by heart. The place we stay in now, it's sort of new, on the outskirts of Lincoln Park. We've only been there a year and a half, and we have these big beautiful trees in front of the house.

We take walks in the evening after dinner. My boys told me that there were bats in the trees, and they shook the trees trying to scare me and I got so mad at them because I'm scared of bats. I like spiders but my daughter has spider-phobia because she was bitten by one. She's not into nature; she's too girly. I try to get her to come out but that's not happening.

My boys would be walking through Washington Park. Mind you, this is a park I used to be scared to go to. I've been slapped on the butt by kids riding bikes, riding past. I've gotten into it with parents about their kids, the things they were doing in the park when we was going to use the park.

But my boys, they got to the point where they loved Washington Park so much, they done caught a couple of young men trying to steal a canoe, and they made them put it back. They caught some boys trying to destroy some of the signs they had just painted and put up; they made them stop.

And I was like, "Wow, I didn't know you guys cared that much."

And that oldest one I have is in competition, him and the youngest one. We'll go out bird watching, but it's a challenge for me. I don't know much and they get mad at me because I can't spot the birds like they can. So, it's almost like a competition, but it's in a fun manner, not in a bad way.

I've been around the UEC about three or four years and they have been nothing but a support system for me. I spoke at two of their solstices. This past solstice, they raised $250,000. When I got off the stage telling my story of how I became a part

Photo courtesy of Katrina Young-Harris

of the Center, I don't think anybody had a dry eye in the house, which was lovely because that's my way of giving back. The solstices are celebrations and also the biggest fundraisers of the year.

I'VE GOT A HUGE SMILE AND I'M NOT DEPRESSED ANYMORE

My boys started with a field trip to the UEC, and from that point on, that's been their after-school activity spot. I did the Food Fridays, fixing a few dishes with the Young Scientists. They cooked, and it was my job to direct them and make sure they were doing everything properly. I also volunteered at the receptionist's desk. When I wasn't working, I would help when they needed volunteers for the mailings.

I tried to get some of the neighborhood kids and their parents to come and volunteer, and see what the kids are doing, so they could be a part of it. I didn't have much luck with that. But I had my mom come with me; that was nice. She was about sixty-five at the time. She helped with a couple of mailings. She was retired, and she enjoyed helping out because it gave her a chance to brag about doing something good. They took our picture and put it in the Urban Ecology Center news-letter—it gave her something to be proud of.

I feel like I'm the poster child for the UEC. I've got a huge smile and I'm not depressed anymore. Now I'm an intern. The stipend is not much, but the experience outweighs the pay. I also am a rental assistant part-time.

When the Center is rented to outside groups, I have the opportunity to let them know if I want to work or not, set up and clean up, and that pays me hourly, which is nice.

I'm a widow. My husband died in 1999 and he was a veteran. I get his pension and his Social Security for myself and the two boys. So, my salary here is like a supplement, otherwise I couldn't afford to work at the UEC, which doesn't pay a lot. I just applied for the volunteer coordinator position at my home base at Washington Park. It's part-time but the pay is good and I want the job and I know I could do it.

I DON'T LIKE BUGS

Since I've started here as an intern, I quit my drug store job that paid eight dollars an hour. I had that job at since I was younger and I didn't mind it. But now that I've gotten older, they wanted to work me too hard at the drug store, so I told them "Goodbye, I'm going to the UEC, I'll take the internship over you guys any day, I think it'll be more beneficial."

My job at the Center has not felt nothing like the drug store; I have had some times where I wanted to pull out my hair at the store. But here, I come in happy and I go home happy. I don't mind being here, I don't mind helping. I am a volunteer visitor service person so I do the receptionist desk, rent out equipment, input data into the computer, clean, make coffee, fill the donut tray and all of that.

I don't like bugs and I have really bad allergies—I just took some Benadryl—from being around a lot of dust and dirt and stuff. But there are things that I will go out and do with the kids, like you know, cleaning up paper around the house, planting stuff, I have no problem with. I feel like if I do one thing, it counts. But I do have allergies so I took the UEC job where I could be on the inside.

PEOPLE SMILE AND IT'S NOT FAKE

I love the Urban Ecology Center, and I'm proud of working here because I come here and people smile and it's not fake, it's genuine. People really do care about the issues, instead of being like politicians who sit and talk about it and get paid to do something to change it, and do nothing but fatten their pockets. Here is my extended family – they're my support system, and I go to them for that. I even have a couple of people I can call at Washington Park if the boys misbehave.

I can call and be like "Please, can you talk to him about so-and-so?"

I've had one of the mentors call me and tell me, "You know, you're wrong."

And it's like, "Huh, those are my children."

And he politely tells me, "No, your boys were all right, you were wrong about them misbehaving."

And I was like, "Oh my God, are you guys growing up somebody else?"

Kids are always way better for other people. Donald is an outdoor leader now, and gets paid more than I do.

I'm so excited about the UEC having three branches. I wish I could have an out-of-body experience and come back in ten years and see if it's going to be three more branches open.

My favorite thing I ever did with the Center was going on the *Denis Sullivan* sailing ship. I had the prettiest white hat on, and the hat blew away in the wind. I lost my thirty-dollar hat, but it didn't matter—I had such a good time on the water. It was a real huge ship, a schooner, with sails and a motor. We were on Lake Michigan right next to the art museum. It was gorgeous. The boys were doing water testing with the UEC and some company from Michigan. The company paid for everybody to go and they invited me.

I BUILT MY OWN GARDEN BOX

I like to plant at home. I built my own eight-foot by ten-foot garden box, inspired by the Center, and I got peppers and greens and tomatoes. I did it myself. I used UEC equipment plus lumber I bought. I used the UEC drill and stuff to put it together. This year we're growing pumpkins and squash.

I have been telling young kids that that there are some cool and amazing things you can find out about nature...the Urban Ecology Center will teach you all you need to know. All you have to do is be willing to learn, because it's here for you, and we're an open community center, so come join us!

MY GREAT-GRANDMA'S COLLARD GREENS RECIPE

Cook two ham hocks in a crock pot one to two hours, for the flavor. You don't eat them. Let the water cook down to about two inches. You don't need a lot of water because greens make their own water. Cook the ham hocks until the tough skin on the exterior is soft.

While the ham hocks are cooking, rinse the collard greens well. Use salt to clean them. The salt kills bugs and loosens dirt. This is an old-fashioned way to clean them that I got from my grandma and she got from her mom. Submerge the greens in the salt water and let them soak. Play with them; that motion in the water will loosen the dirt and get the bugs out. Cut off the spine like you cut off a kale spine, keeping just a small portion of spine right before it gets too thick.

Chop the clean greens before you cook them.

Add greens to the water. Keep the ham hocks in with them. Cook them for three to four hours, adding salt to season to taste.

At the end, discard the ham hocks. Chop onions and add them for flavor, like a topping.

The water left in the pot is called "pot liquor." You get a lot of vitamins and nutrients from that pot liquor.

ANYTHING YOU CAN CONTRIBUTE, IT HELPS

It's important for all of us to learn how to preserve nature for the future, so there's still beautiful and healthy things left for your kids or my grandkids or whoever comes next. We want to be able to teach and show them something that we did that was positive instead of doing damage.

It only takes a little bit. You don't have to go out and do gigantic projects or anything. Anything you can contribute, it helps. Because like me, I go pick up paper in the neighborhoods. I hate for paper to be in front of my house; it irks me. I feel like just by me picking up that one piece of paper, I'm making a difference. Even if it don't do nothing else, I'm making a difference.

Since I got involved with the UEC, I've been getting out the house more than I ever had before. Those were some deep, dark times for me and it was like the sun just shined in and said "Girl, you've got to get up, you've got to do something differ- ent, you can't wallow in it, you've got to get out of it." And that's exactly what I did.

I'M SO EXTREMELY PROUD

I think that nature will help mold and shape young people's career path, because it's done that for my boys. Donovin wants to be an oceanographer and I already told you that Donald wants to be an ornithologist. They didn't want that before they started being a part of the Center. I'm so proud, I'm so extreme- ly proud, that I don't even know what to do.

If they open up Urban Ecology Centers in different cities, I would love if they offered me a good-paying job. I would move with and take my boys right along with me. Yes, yes, yes. I would like to see UECs in different parts of the world, too. People have been calling the Center to see how they can get the same thing going on in their city.

I want the UEC to grow, grow, grow, grow. Get more and more and more people involved. I did their last mailing. They have close to 3,000 members. I would like to see that number double. I would like to see more people come out and get involved, make a difference. I want our world to be better. Just to sum that up, to be better.

Donald Harris (15 years old at time of interview)

"We know that crime is down in Riverside Park by over 90% since we first started running programs there, and is down by nearly 60% since we started operating in Washington Park in 2007."
—Ken Leinbach,
*Urban Ecology: A Natural Way to Transform
Kids, Parks, Cities, and the World*

DONALD HARRIS: "I'M NOT TOO COOL FOR THIS AFTER ALL."

IT'S CALLED A DIRT CAKE EVEN THOUGH THERE'S NO CAKE ABOUT IT

My life before I got involved with the Urban Ecology Center was basically school, chores at home, and an after-school program at my school, or going to the library.

I went to Neeskara School on 55th and Vliet. The stuff I did there was kind of environmental. In the winter, we had big snowball fights, but we had to stop that because it was too dangerous. Now you can get suspended or expelled for throwing snowballs, because sometimes some people put rocks into the snowballs.

In warm weather at Neeskara, we helped out with the gardens. I thought gardening was fun. And then at harvest time, we had a big garden party with the stuff that we grew. Our dessert was a big barrel full of pudding with Oreos and gummi worms—it's called a dirt cake even though there's no cake about it—we ate it. The parents came and they ate it, too.

DIRT UNDER MY FINGERNAILS

I was about four or five the very first time I went to the Urban Ecology Center from my school. At the time, I really wasn't paying attention, but I did like the Center.

The time when I really got interested in nature and the Center, both, was when I was at Westside Academy. I was probably like eight years old. We went on a field trip to the Washington Park branch of the UEC. We walked from our school since our school was just down the way, and planted flowers in a rain garden. I got dirt under my fingernails but it didn't bother me. The flowers are still there.

My family had moved from our old house and we were still going to the same school. One day we got a letter saying they were having an Earth Day at the UEC. That's when it really started, because when we came, me and my mom (page 116) and my brother, we had a great time. One of the staff, I don't remember who it was, he encouraged me to come back. After that, I started coming to the UEC regularly.

Someone at the Center told my mom about the Young Scientists Club and gave us an application and she signed it. Two days after Earth Day, we came on a Tuesday at 4:00 o'clock and we went canoeing. I was about nine and that was my first Young Scientist experience.

I WAS SCARED

I'll never forget when I was in a canoe for the first time in my life. I was sitting in the back of the canoe and I was scared, even though they taught me about paddling before I got in. There were about ten or eleven kids in the group and we canoed to the island. We got out of the canoes and went onto the island. First, we just chilled on the island while we listened to the leader talk about it. Then we made a hut out of sticks. It's still there. It's just a bunch of branches, not a real hut, but it's made into kind of like a half-hut. Every time you visit the island, you'll notice that the hut is changed because people keep building on it.

After that, we canoed back to the Center and we talked about stuff that we saw on the island, bugs and plants and different stuff, and then we left for home. My brother Donovin was with me. He's a year younger. He's not as focused on nature as me, but I don't feel like he's not as passionate as me about it. When we got home that day, we told our mom that we had fun and we wanted to go back. And we just kept going back every day. Sometimes I'd stay longer than the Young Scientist hours, but no one told me I had to leave.

PEOPLE USED TO BE AFRAID TO CROSS

I'm fifteen now, and I haven't really stopped coming since then. I went from participant to volunteer to employee; it was kind of a natural evolution. When people volunteer, they're participants too. Gradually you get more and more responsibility. Even though I'm an employee, I've been here so long that it doesn't feel much different. It's like I'm getting paid to do stuff that I'd do anyway. Everyone is always learning at the Urban Ecology Center; it doesn't matter if you're a volunteer or an employee.

I'm an outdoor leader. Here at the Washington Park location, we have a variety of children that come. At Riverside Park, it's little kids in the Young Scientists programs, and older folks. At Menomonee Valley, they have a mixed variety of ages like at Washington Park, but that's still a new branch. They're doing well. We're getting people more involved in Menomonee Valley because people used to be afraid in that area to cross the 35th Street viaduct. Adults would tell their kids not to cross the bridge.

I love going on trips with the Center. People just stare at our bus—it's decorated with animals. Some people will be taking pictures of the bus, and then I see them go on their phone, probably trying to punch in the UEC phone number.

(Photo courtesy of Donald Harris)

CRAY AIKENS AND CRAY MATTHEWS

From a science standpoint, it's two things I'm interested in. I used to like geology before even coming here; that's why I used to go to the library, to look up geology and stuff like that. And then I got into ornithology and so it's kind of like a battle between those two, and astronomy—I like astronomy as well—but I like the two main ones, ornithology and geology, the most. Erick Anderson (page 142), who works here, jokes that I want to be an ornithologist and a geologist so I can kill two birds with one stone.

From another standpoint, I kind of like aquatic stuff, because I really like crayfish. People say I'm obsessed with crayfish. I used to name them. At Washington Park, we had Cray and Cray Aikens and Cray Matthews.

I like to look at them and take care of them. We had a tank down in the basement especially made for crayfish. It was an old tank and the crayfish escaped because they climbed onto the filter – it was like a cut that you slipped the filter into. We used to have a bunch of them living in our filter. They weren't meant to go into the filter. But unfortunately, one time they climbed up the filter and escaped and dried up before they found water.

Just one crayfish had survived, but a kid at the Center fed it to the snapping turtle. He did it on purpose. He took it out of the tank and gave it to Jaws, the snapping turtle, and Jaws ate it. But I think the crayfish had been pregnant and had laid her eggs because some of the eggs had got into the filter. Later, when we came back to the UEC, there was a bunch of crayfish in there. We had to get them all out because it was dangerous for them in the filter.

NATURE BECAME MY LIFE DIRECTION

The Urban Ecology Center was something that me and my mom and my brother could do together, and it was free and educational. It changed my mom, the way she cooked, for one. When she came here, she saw what people cooked from the UEC garden and she got a few ideas for food. She makes it to her own style now. She'll add more vegetable stuff or do more combinations of vegetable stuff.

We have Food Fridays here, a big meal for the staff and the kids, where we eat from the gardens that we plant. I think the first thing we made from the garden was something with beans and peppers, in tacos or something like that. I don't think it was a stir fry at first. The bean thing happened because of some vegetarian people. We still have vegetarian people, that's why Food Fridays aren't always meat, not always vegetables. I think stir fry came in a few weeks later, once Food Friday got more solid, when people started asking to have it.

It was two times my mom helped at Food Fridays. The first time, she made pasta and then the second time she made her special thing, rotelle. It's like a meat-nacho thing. We took peppers and stuff from the garden and we ate it. But she said she won't do another one until we get a new stove here.

Nature became my life direction. It wasn't that way before, like it is now. I want to go to college for environmental education and science. Diondre got me into it. I can't say I influenced my brother; he just came when he could come. I influenced my mom and a couple of my friends and some other people to get involved with nature.

I worked on a research project called "Driven to Discover." There were three girls involved on the project who didn't care about birds. They still only kind of do, but I think they saw my passion for doing the research, and that might have helped them want to join. We all got the ego trip out of going to a big conference and getting recognized.

We had three different projects: one in the first year we did together as a group, me and one other guy and three girls. We compared birds from the shoreline of Washington Park to the island of Washington Park. We had one group go out to the island and do a bird count and we had the other group do a bird count on the land. We wanted to see how many bird species we could find and how many of each species we could find and we compared those.

The second year, we did a project in two separate groups, and this time it was more people. I was a volunteer at the time, about fourteen years old, and Erick Anderson asked me to see if anybody else would be interested in this. So, I asked some people in the Young Scientists club would they like to do it, and they said yes. My group consisted of me and five others. The other group had about five kids in it.

Besides the members of the Young Scientists club, the other ones were volunteers like me and Donovin. We called ourselves Youth Volunteers. Eventually most of the guys dropped out of the project; summer camp and summer school were the two main reasons. My brother thought he was cool and plus he had summer camp. So, it was just me and Liam [Lee, page 176) and quite a few girls who finished the work.

People who thought they were too cool for it saw us get to go to Minnesota for the project. Then they realized, "Oh! I'm not too cool for this after all."

The second year, we started with mini-projects to see if we still knew how to go from a hypothesis to procedure, stuff like that. They were just testing us, seeing if we still knew how to do it on our own. We split up into four groups. I did a regular bird count in Washington Park in spring. Then Marie's group, she did a survey about what people were doing in the park: were they fishing, running their dogs, walking, biking? The other group did a bird count as well. And the fourth group did something else.

I took the bird count and Marie's idea and I said, "What activities are birds doing in Washington Park? Are they perched or on the lagoon or on the land or in the sky?" Those were the four things—it was a count of birds and what they were doing.

We went to Minnesota both years, to the conference. There were small gatherings in various rooms, with a panel of scientists and some kids. We got to hear other people's projects and present our own. The main thing the projects were about was bugs - monarchs, butterflies, and some invertebrates. We were one of eleven projects to do birds.

In Minnesota, we stayed in a hotel, and that was fun. We went swimming. We ate a lot of candy, I mean, like too much candy. We had a whole jar of Laffy Taffy, the little sticks, and I brought my chocolate and stuff. That time, we had a van. That van had a lot of trash on the floor. But we cleaned it up.

This is the third year of the project. I came up with the idea to study the population of Canadian geese affecting the population of migrating species. We haven't started that yet.

ALL YOU NEED IS JUST ONE PERSON
TO HELP YOU OR GUIDE YOU

I think people should care about nature because it's an important tool and an important resource. Not only that, you don't want to leave it vulnerable. You want the future generations to be able to use it or see it. Unless you get to know nature better and help it, you'll see nature as a whole different thing. Like say, we take you on a bird walk in Washington Park, for your first time, and you'll see little things you never noticed.

All you need is just one person to help you or guide you to experience something so you can better understand nature – and that's what they did at the UEC. They guided me through it, and now I know nature more than if I wouldn't have experienced the Center. I wouldn't see or notice the little things that I do. Appreciating nature makes my life happier because I know it's things I can do besides sit in the park and watch people.

I feel like video games is just a thing that you can do. I can see if you don't want to go outside maybe because it's cold. All you need is somebody to influence you to go outside. You don't need nobody to influence you to play video games; you're going to play games anyway. All you need is just one person to ask you to come outside. Most people love to go outside if they just do it—it's the thing about having someone there to go outside with.

I got into Escuela Verde. It's on the south side, on 1st and Mineral Street, I think. It's a nature lovers' school, kind of a free environment, sort of like the Urban Ecology Center. It's a project-based, green high school. I don't know that much about it but I know that it's a good school. I've been into the school and I like the feel of it. I like that no one's forcing us to do anything and we help make decisions on what we do. It's self-led; you don't get led by anyone else. They put you at the level where you test in. I'm in tenth grade but at that school, I'll be in eleventh grade because I do eleventh grade work. That's the work I did at Milwaukee Public Schools.

My brother Donovin and my friend Gustave are also going to go to Escuela Verde next school year. They both have been part of the UEC Young Scientists club for years. If I just keep doing what I did at MPS, or if I do a little bit better, I'll be out of high school at age sixteen or seventeen.

I wish for the Urban Ecology Center to keep going as long as possible, plus I want the Center to influence other organizations, not necessarily to make another UEC because I don't think there can be another UEC, but I feel like that we can help influence people.

If people like to travel, I suggest getting into nature. Nature is not just in one place; it's everywhere. I love traveling. I've been to Atlanta, Chicago, Michigan, DC, Virginia and New York outside the UEC. With the UEC, I've been to Minnesota, Chicago, New York, North Carolina, Michigan, Iowa, and places around Wisconsin. I went backpacking with the Center in Michigan. When I travel, I try to see nature. Sometimes I go to sleep, though. I like looking at farmland and seeing different parts of each state when I travel. When I'm looking at farmland, it's relaxing so I just kind of fall asleep.

My wish for the world is that people who think nature is dangerous or people who don't get involved in nature, and the big wigs, people with money, would get more involved – not spending money, just go out into nature, experience nature, don't judge what you see outside as something negative, just take the goodness of everything and experience, explore. And if it is negative, then I ask that you make a donation to help make it better because it is your place where you work and you visit. It is yours and everyone else's land.

PS DATED AUGUST 2016

I'm seventeen now. I graduated from Escuela Verde in June, a year early, and I'll be starting college at the University of Wisconsin–Stevens Point in September. I'm pretty happy about that. I am going to college on the GI bill because my father was in the service.

I finished up my internship as an outdoor leader at the Urban Ecology Center. Life at the UEC is great, and I'll be connected with the Center during college and even after. Some staff said they'll come up and visit me at Stevens Point and send care packages.

I'll also stay connected with Escuela Verde. I'll be in touch with some of the staff and students, and I'll see them when they come visit me during their yearly field trips to Stevens Point. I'll visit Escuela Verde when I'm home on break.

My mom is happy I graduated early and she's happy I'm going to college.

I want to do a double major in water ecology and biology. With biology, I'll still have some ornithology in there. I'm not sure yet but I'm thinking about a minor in archeological studies.

After college, there are research jobs affecting the Great Lakes and environmental issues with water that the world faces. Or I might take my skills back to Milwaukee to help with the ecological situations that we face.

(Photo courtesy of Donald Harris)

Canoeing on the lagoon in Washington Park
(Photo courtesy of the Urban Ecology Center)

Erick Anderson, 30 years old at time of interview
(Photo courtesy of Erick Anderson)

"We know, from surveys, that over 90% of the students who come through our programs learned something, had fun, gained a deeper appreciation for nature, and would recommend the program to a friend."

—Ken Leinbach,
Urban Ecology: A Natural Way to Transform
Kids, Parks, Cities, and the World

ERICK ANDERSON: "FEAR DOESN'T MOTIVATE ME; PASSION DOES, EMPATHY DOES."

I KNEW I SHOULD CARE ABOUT THE ENVIRONMENT, BUT I DIDN'T REALLY KNOW HOW

I had very little environmental background other than going outside and hiking and canoeing when I was a kid, with my family. I did a lot outside but I couldn't identify plants or any of that yet.

When I first came to the Urban Ecology Center, I had just graduated from college. I was at the point in my life where I had to figure out what I was going to do with myself. My initial plan had been to be a high school science teacher, so I studied chemistry, physics, secondary education. I didn't feel ready to go into classroom teaching right after I graduated. I didn't finish my teaching license at that point. I'd planned on maybe coming back and finishing it in a few years. I was weighing a couple of different options after I graduated.

I could have worked as a chemist but I also wanted to try a volunteer program like AmeriCorps or Peace Corps. I had a science background and I had experience working with kids; I worked at a summer camp for many years. I ended up applying for Lutheran Volunteer Corps, which is the program that placed me at the UEC as an educator.

I was at the Riverside branch, a year before the Washington Park branch opened, eight years ago. I was enrolled in Ameri-Corps concurrently with Lutheran Volunteer Corps. This is a program that places people at not-for-profits around the city and they all live in a house together for a year. I did that for two years. There were six people in the house during my first year, seven during my second year. We lived in the neighborhood just west of the park, Washington Heights, in a church parson-age on 55th and Lloyd Streets. We each had our own job that we worked at full time, at different not-for-profits around the city.

I didn't have much of an environmental ethic before then. I hadn't been exposed to it. It wasn't that I didn't care about the environment; I knew I should care about the environment, in theory, but I didn't really know how. It never occurred to me that biking to work was a good idea, or eating less meat or eating organic food might be worth considering—it was never a part of my reality. I had an environmental ethic in a sense, like I saw *An Inconvenient Truth*, and all that. I knew that environ-mental disaster is out there, the rainforest is being depleted, all the environmental disaster stuff you learn about in school, but I was lacking the personal connection.

It's been such an important part of our culture here at the UEC that it helped me learn. The Center made me care about it and gave me a reason to care. That's an important part of our whole educational philosophy here. Fear has never been a motivator for me. Fear doesn't motivate me to do anything. Passion does. Empathy does.

I CAN BIKE TO WORK. OKAY, THIS IS HARD-CORE

With biking for example, as first it was something new and fun. Like I can bike to work. Okay, this is hard-core. Not a lot of people do that, so it was something I could brag about, and it's exercise. But the more I did it, I started thinking creatively about it, like "Why is this important? At least I'm not using gasoline. Why does that matter? Every trip I'm taking on my bike is gas I'm not using and pollution I'm not generating." That made it more appealing. Those environmental factors weren't enough to motivate me in the first place, but after I got motivated to do it, then I started to realize, "Oh, this is an action that's having a positive effect on the environment. This is good. I should keep doing this."

I didn't even have a car for those two years in Lutheran Volunteer Corps. I never would have thought to do that, other than all my co-workers were doing that, and I thought, *Cool.* In winter, I took the bus mostly, which is awesome. I always liked people-watching. There are interesting people on the bus. Depending on which bus you ride, there are people from all walks of life. You'll be riding through downtown to get to the Center, you'll be riding with a lot of professionals. There are people from other neighborhoods together.

This is a lot easier to do before you have a kid you have to drop off at daycare every day. I have a child now who is sixteen months old.

It's what kids should be able to do

As part of my job with the UEC, I have worked with many schools. My wife is a Milwaukee Public Schools nurse at Golda Meir School, and she told me that district-wide at MPS, if you throw a snowball, you can be suspended. I kind of get it to an extent. I had a debate with her about this. She's a nurse who deals with kids getting hurt from stuff like this, but I think you should be able to throw a snowball. It's what kids should be able to do. I think of all the times I've brought kids on field trips and watched them throw snowballs. I'm wondering how mortified were the teachers about this. I would have never even thought that throwing snowballs was a problem.

The only time we kick people out of the building is when we have to close

My job for my first five years here was working with primary neighborhood schools. Neeskara School is one of our partner schools for our NEEP program, our school field trips. NEEP stands for the Neighborhood Environmental Education Project. Any UEC branch partners with public and private schools in a two-mile radius if they're interested. Here at Washington Park, we have more schools that are interested than we can fit into our schedule. We have a waiting list. There's something like one hundred schools within our two-mile radius here.

I think at Menomonee Valley, they've maxed out their current capacity for staff but they've built into their overall plan to eventually hire more staff and offer more programming. Riverside I think has a little bit more capacity as well, that would require hiring more people. I'm pretty sure we've maxed out all the contracts for buses and staff and space.

I remember this time when I was driving back from Clarke Street School after I dropped a group off there. I was driving the UEC van that is all decorated with animals, down Center Street, at a stoplight, and this guy pulls up on my right and beeps his horn and motions at me to roll down my window. I thought he was going to yell at me for something.

I opened my window and talked to him and he said, "Hey, UEC, I love that place. I went there when I was a kid!"

I thought, *Yeah, all right!*

The only time we kick people out of the building is when we have to close, because we want to go home. Other than that, if kids are being respectful, we're okay with them being around, even if we're not in the official Young Scientist hours.

About three years ago or so, the previous coordinator, Scott, built these learning gardens out in front of the building. When I first started leading Young Scientists, I realized we had all this food to harvest and I needed something to do with these kids, so I said, "Let's go outside, let's pick some food, and then we'll cook something." I didn't put a whole lot of fore-thought into it; it just seemed like a convenient thing to do. And the kids loved it.

Donald (page 128) and Donovin Harris were there the first time we did it. And they were all over it. And I was like, "Okay, let's try it again next week." We have to do garden maintenance every week, we can try it again. We'll do it on Fridays. It took off from there. It became a regular program, something we advertise in our newsletter, with a grant now that funds it during the summer.

THE GIRLS TOTALLY OUTNUMBERED THE GUYS

There was a University of Minnesota program called "Driven to Discover." They have a grant from the National Science Foundation, and the purpose of the grant is to get kids involved in citizen science. I got invited to attend their adult leader training on how to facilitate this program. We thought it might be a good fit with Washington Park Young Scientists club. I came back from the training and I picked out certain members of the Young Scientists club who I thought would be a good fit for a bird survey of Washington Park.

One of the best things that came out of this, quite honestly, is I've always felt like we've had a harder time engaging girls than guys in the Young Scientists program. Until now, the leaders have always been guys. What came out of this project is most of the guys quit except for Donald and Liam (Lee, page 176)—they're the only ones who stuck with it, so it was these guys and the ladies. The girls totally outnumbered the guys. The project got them more engaged. We got to go to Minnesota to show our results. These were easy trips to facilitate. The kids were so well-behaved and respectful. We're in the third year of the project now.

YOU GO HOME AND PLAY VIDEO GAMES, YOU'RE GOOD

Kids come to the Center, go outside, then go home and still get to play video games. That's important to me. I don't like this notion that it's nature versus video games. I mean, all these guys play video games. I do; I grew up playing video games. I think making kids feel bad about playing video games is not something I'm about. You come here, you go outside, you go home and play video games, you're good. Just make sure you're getting outside.

A GRADE-SCHOOLER VERSUS A MIDDLE-SCHOOLER IS WAY DIFFERENT

I've been here just about eight years now, since 2006. I'm a community program coordinator. That means I'm in charge of

Urban Ecology Center Washington Park
(Photo courtesy of Sarina Counard-Ryals)

all the programs that happen on the evenings and weekends at the UEC Washington Park. I basically act like second in charge. I supervise our community program educator and coordinate all those educational programs. I either lead them or have educators Rachel and Kirsten lead them. I supervise them and they take leadership. I also supervise the high school outdoor leaders; Donald Harris is now one of them.

Washington Park is a place you wouldn't go to or think of going to if you didn't know it was there. There are certain programs that happen at all three branches, but because of the nature of our programs, they have a different feel to them. Summer camps and our school programs are pretty similar across all our three branches. Our after-school Young Scientists clubs are at all three branches, but the character is very different based on the neighborhoods. At Riverside, it's mostly younger kids who have gotten really engaged in the after-school Young Scientists club, talking about six-, seven-, eight-year-olds. It's one of the ways we engage neighborhood kids, drop-in kids.

I think where we've really had success at Washington Park is keeping them engaged as they got older, which isn't easy. Engaging a grade schooler versus a middle schooler is way different. Trying to engage both ages at the same time in the same program can be really challenging. It's a challenge that we've embraced and rolled with. We've been really successful; we've had a core of kids.

Donald Harris started coming when he was nine or ten and he's fifteen now, and he hasn't really stopped coming during that time. He went from participant to volunteer to employee, and there's never been a strict delineation between those three; it's kind of a natural evolution. As a volunteer, you're a participant too. Gradually you get more and more responsibility. And now Donald works here, but he's been here so long it probably doesn't feel any different. It's like he's getting paid to do stuff that he'd do anyway. We're all always learning here.

IT TOOK A LOT OF FORESIGHT... TO MAKE SURE THAT EVERY NEIGHBORHOOD HAD AT LEAST ONE PARK

Something I've come to appreciate in my time at the Center is how much nature you can experience without traveling much at all. Our County Parks system is awesome. It took a lot of foresight back in the 1920s and 30s when the city and county were being developed, to set aside that land and make sure that every neighborhood had at least one park. I'm glad that happened. Nationally, Milwaukee has one of the most respected park systems, deservedly so.

WE'VE HAD THIS CULTURE OF POSITIVITY AND OPENNESS

There's a lot we do at the Urban Ecology Center, and a lot more we can do. We've grown immensely in the time I've been here. I think what's always in the forefront of my mind is making sure that as we continue to grow and do more with new people, we don't lose the feel and culture that's been really important to me. It's hard to maintain our culture as we get bigger, but we have.

We've had this culture of positivity and openness that brought us to where we are. It's a good place to work and makes people like us, just the way we treat them and our employees and others in our community. We're successful because of that. If we stop treating people well, we won't be successful. My wish is to make sure that no matter what happens in our organization, we always treat people with kindness and respect as we always have, and we influence other people to do that as well.

I WANT MY CHILD TO HAVE A PLACE WHERE HE CAN PLAY OUTSIDE

I think ultimately what motivates me to do what I do is I want to see people be good people. I want kids to grow up to be good people. Nature is a means that we accomplish that. It's as much about people for me as about nature. My wish for the environment is that I want my child to be able to grow up and have a place where he can play outside with other kids, and they can play together and have fun together. That's what's most important to me.

Ice skating at Washington Park
(Photo courtesy of the Urban Ecology Center)

Darrin Madison, 19 years old at time of interview
(Photo courtesy of Darrin Madison)

"Trees breathe in carbon dioxide and breathe out life-supporting oxygen, which is so important in urban environments. But breathing space is needed also in a metaphorical sense. Parks are places where a person can breathe and mentally relax. Our brains have evolved for 70 million years to relax among the plants and abundant life of a vibrant ecosystem. Nature is so crucial to our beings and our health."
—Ken Leinbach,
Urban Ecology: A Natural Way to Transform
Kids, Parks, Cities, and the World

DARRIN MADISON:
NATURE IS A PLAYGROUND

*IT'S THE LITTLE THINGS THAT MAKE YOU
REALIZE YOU LOVE NATURE*

I was raised in the HiMount Boulevard neighborhood in the inner city of Milwaukee. I went to Ronald Reagan College Prep High School.

I first went to the Urban Ecology Center when I was nine or ten years old, the first year the Washington Park branch was established. Before that, I wasn't really exposed to nature; it wasn't a huge interest. I knew about nature, but I felt indifferent.

This is how I discovered the UEC: I was hanging out at the Washington Park library. I was leaving the library and I saw a friend with a group of kids in Washington Park, playing Frisbee. My friend asked me to join them and I decided I wanted to play. Scott was the coordinator and he invited me to the Center.

So, I go back inside and see this amazing animal room, all these snakes and frogs and turtles. Daniel Rawley (page 184) had a snake around his neck. He asked me if I wanted to hold it. I was super frightened and really excited. I never saw a snake before. I held the snake and realized how much I loved nature.

It's the little things that make you realize you love nature.

I kept coming back. I helped do water testing and I played so many different games. I went sledding, tapped maple trees. I asked friends if they wanted to see some cool animals. They came for about three years. We went sledding together, went fishing, did research. Eventually they lost interest, but I didn't.

YOU CAN CUT A BASKETBALL IN HALF TO USE AS A POOL

During high school, I worked with the Urban Underground (UU). I first discovered it through the Urban Ecology Center. I helped facilitate volunteer work and learned more about UU. It's a youth leadership organization that teaches youth they have a voice and how to use their voice in their communities. When I was sixteen, I worked with some other members of the UU to write a grant to start a campaign called "Fresh Plates." The idea was that people would learn about agriculture in today's society.

The campaign focused on bringing fresh food to urban food deserts around Milwaukee's underprivileged neighbor-hoods. The goals were to eat fresh food, grow fresh food, and buy fresh food. We worked on teaching people how to make dishes that they already eat in healthier and affordable ways. We focused on trying to establish cooperation between communities to have systems focused on organic food: having community gardens and using the grant money to fund more initiatives with different ways to grow things. For example, you can cut a basketball in half to use as a pool in your garden.

Fondy Food Market and Alice's Garden in Milwaukee are examples of people bringing fresh food into urban areas. At the Linden Sculpture Garden in Brown Deer, a New York artist built a research garden with an aquaponics system. It's still there.

Last year, a group of young people in the Urban Underground wanted to do work for an online blog series featuring organic recipes.

I'm still part of the UU. You can see the work of the organization on You Tube videos. Whenever I'm in Milwaukee, I join in and do things that the UU is doing with high school students.

WE WERE WORKING LIKE SCIENTISTS

Some summers at the UEC, they were examining different invertebrates found in nature. We were doing netting, looking at all these invertebrates, seeing how they are in their environment. You can use invertebrates to find information about water quality. You look at these little invertebrates under a microscope...it's like they have their own universe.

I looked at what is the life cycle of these invertebrates. We were looking at damsel fly larvae under a microscope, but we couldn't figure out what it was. We had a key to identifying invertebrates. We'd look at the checklist to identify it: How many legs? Antennae? Wings? How many? Scott helped me. It was like a maze to pinpoint the unidentified organism—we were working like scientists.

When you're trying to figure out what you want to do in life, it's these moments that influence you.

THEY'RE MORE CONCERNED ABOUT THEIR OWN LACK OF RESOURCES

It's really hard to get people you don't know interested in nature. It's easier with people you hang out with. Even one time in nature can make a huge difference in someone's interest. "You can lead a horse to water, but you can't make him drink."

This is a huge issue for young people, especially people in the Inner City. Not knowing that opportunities are there or not having access to amazing experiences is a huge dividing line that keeps young people from experiencing nature. When you're talking to people who are underprivileged about nature and resources, they're more concerned about their own lack of resources.

That's what I liked about the outdoor leader program at the Urban Ecology Center. You'd go on an outdoor leader retreat for two weeks in the Porcupine Mountains. If you didn't love nature before, you would after that.

"I'M GOING TO DECLARE IT AS MY SPIRIT ANIMAL"

One of my favorite memories is from Wyoming, in Yellowstone Park. We had spent the day climbing Specimen Peak. On the way up, one of the outdoor leaders was having an issue because he was scared of heights. We all slowed down; we were supportive and we helped him. Once we were on the top, we were overlooking this amazing valley. We could see a pronghorn sheep running around, and green minerals and copper under our feet. Somebody found a topaz sample. Finally, the guy who was scared felt better, once he was up on top of the peak. Going down, it was hard again.

Then we found some bison poop. We had a stick and we were playing baseball with it. We camped in tents and we also stayed at Teton Science School. We spent the night in Mammoth Springs, camping out. Again, the pronghorns were really close to our tents. We looked at the stars and had a conversation about the universe and how big it is.

Seeing all the geysers in Wyoming, all the color changes from the heat and bacteria in the geysers, was amazing. They change color, all the colors of the rainbow. The blues are where it is hotter. It was amazing to see how liquid goes through all those different tunnel systems formed over millions of years.

I was about seventeen for that trip to Wyoming. There was one amazing moment when we were walking through the Tetons. I was talking about "If I see a moose, I'm going to declare it as my spirit animal." Right after that, we saw a moose through the trees. We made jokes about it.

CHANGES IN MY FAMILY

At the Center, I started as a volunteer, then worked as a Young Scientist, and eventually became an outdoor leader. Young Scientists exposed me to those things I would have never seen: how to take care of animals, water testing, and identifying invertebrates. These awesome experiences pre-exposed me to things that could enable me to go on to biological research or zoology. My dream job is to be an environmental lawyer with the Environmental Protection Agency.

My experiences have led to some changes in my family. I have brought some recipes home and cooked for them occasionally. I've made small organic meals, like stir fries, for my mom and two older brothers and my younger brother and sister.

THE PEOPLE HELPED PLANT APPLE TREES

I go to Howard University in Washington DC. I believe it was the first big black college established in America. It has a biology program. I'm trying for a double major, in political science and biology. I plan to go into environmental law. A lot of being at Howard is being in DC. There are many opportunities for students who want to do environmental work. My friend is doing an internship with the Environmental Protection Agency. I'm hoping to get that internship. I've been talking to one of their environmental lawyers.

I've also been working with other students, trying to establish an environmental nonprofit on campus. Technically it would be a club, but being a nonprofit through the university, we could get grant funds. There's a huge issue of urban food deserts especially in the neighborhood surrounding Howard University.

My wish for the Urban Ecology Center is mostly for more resources for Washington Park. I love the UEC but there could have been more involvement from the community around Washington Park. It was wonderful when the people from the community helped plant apple trees there. It was during the same summer that the father of one of the Young Scientists passed away. One of the trees was dedicated to him.

WE DON'T NEED ASPHALT AND METAL TO HAVE FUN

I wish that people had a better appreciation for natural resources, because they're being depleted. The only things that can reduce the depletion of resources are the ones causing it—which is us.

My ideal world would have fewer water pollutants, especially in Lake Michigan, and more trees in neighborhoods. Ideally, they'd be fruit trees. It would be amazing to have apple trees all around. We need natural places that young people can play in. We don't need asphalt and metal to have fun. Nature is a playground. Everybody would have access to fresh produce, there would be more fresh and organic produce, and prices would decrease.

Jennifer Johnson, 19 years old at time of interview
(Photo courtesy of Jennifer Johnson)

"When discovering is encouraged, there is greater engagement with the natural world, and greater potential change and connection and care within a neighborhood and between species."
—Ken Leinbach,
Urban Ecology: A Natural Way to Transform
Kids, Parks, Cities, and the World

Jennifer Johnson:
"Bam, it connects!"

I DIDN'T HEAR THE BIRDS

I was not much interested in nature as a kid. I liked to go outside, but I didn't pay close attention. I would pick flowers and give them to my mom. I always hated litter. I loved sports, I wanted to be with my friends and family, I liked movies and the mall, and I liked to sleep. As far as nature, I feel like I'm drawing a blank because it wasn't really an aspect. You know, I'd go to a park for a barbecue, I loved music and I heard the music going but I didn't hear the birds.

When I was little, I thought about gardening fresh crops, and I just assumed that wasn't in the city; it was in suburbs and farms. My aunt had a garden in Ohio, but that was in the suburbs, in her back yard. In the inner city, there's not a lot of back yards.

I liked going to the beach—that was my idea of nature. Scratch going in the woodland or prairie—those words were never in my vocabulary—or vernal ponds—never in my vocabulary at all, I did not know about them. Maybe prairie… maybe. But everything else, no. Beach was my nature.

EVEN LIVE FISH ARE CREEPY TO ME

I discovered the Urban Ecology Center during the summer of 2011, when I became an outdoor leader. I didn't know anything about the Center; I just wanted the job. I did the interview but I had no idea that I did well on it.

My first job was with the UEC. I was fifteen, and it was a paid summer internship that extended into a yearlong position. I worked at summer camps at Riverside. During my yearlong position, I came to Washington Park to help with outdoor activities with the Young Scientists club after school. I helped maintain the animal room; other outdoor leaders were pros in there. I led water safety courses and worked with volunteer groups. There were many possibilities for me.

Erick Anderson (page 142) was so helpful. He does all in his power to help someone. He quickly identifies your strengths and gives a leadership position according to your strength. He let me take volunteer groups to the park, and do ice breakers with them. It was teen-run. And Erick challenges your weaknesses.

My weakness: I am deathly afraid of dead fish. Even live fish are creepy to me. Erick put me on feeding fish and cleaning tanks. I looked at Erick and said, "I can't do this." Erick and I debated about five minutes. Then he said, "You can do it," and handed me a sponge. He's my boss. I scrubbed algae off rocks in the turtle tank, then in the fish tank. I stood on a stool and reached to the bottom. There was a largemouth bass named Roy who was mean, and also a perch in the tank. I scrubbed the rocks until Roy got too close.

I was a little stern with kids at first. Erick pulled me into the office and talked to me about it. He explained that kids are so ready to have fun; they're not being rude. Now I have more patience.

EVERYONE GENUINELY CARES

I've very family-oriented. I form quick bonds—I'm emotional about Willie leaving the Center. Everyone here is so genuine. Everyone genuinely cares about nature and the people we encounter. It's unbelievable the feeling you get when you walk in here. Members and volunteers say the same thing. Each branch has a different feeling.

I live on the south side, but I can't get enough of Washington Park, which is on the north side.

There are scholarships for summer camps—we want everybody to come. We're really good at inclusivity. We need everybody—all ages, races, economic statuses. We have some contributing memberships, where we accept winter clothes or volunteer time instead of cash.

HOME-GROWN FOOD IN THE CITY

Kids come in from the neighborhood, they want something to do, they want something positive. We always try to put the community first even though we might have other stuff to do. One morning, I drove up the service road at 9:00 am and I saw a bunch of kids. They were about age seven through thirteen. "Where are your parents?" I asked them. The kids told me the parents were asleep. I invited them in and showed them the animal room. I let them hold the snakes. One girl seemed scared of getting a poisonous snake bite. I taught her the difference between venom and poison. She held the snake eventually. I taught her that the snakes here are friendly. All her siblings touched the snake.

In the learning gardens, kids choose what they'll plant. They plant everything, tend it, pick it, and choose how they'll cook it. Like they'll make mint tea lemonade, for example. This summer, I was looking outside at the gardens and I saw a boy pulling crops up. I didn't want to go out and yell at him; I didn't want his first impression of the Center to be yelling.

I walked outside and just said, "Hey!"

He looked scared, like he saw a ghost.

I said, "Why don't we look at the gardens?" We looked at them together. I asked him, "What is it?"

He said, "I don't know."

That's why he pulled the stuff. He thought it was weeds. We picked mint and replanted what he had pulled.

I told him, "Kids grow this."

He told me he was thirteen and lived in the area. I brought him into the animal room, then showed him the canoes and kayaks. I told him about what we do. He said, "Oh, it's so cool." He loved the tandem kayak. He wanted to ride the tandem with his parents around the lagoon.

I asked him if he was interested in volunteering. That day he started volunteering, picking up trash around and in the lagoon. He launched a canoe and got a ride with an intern. They picked up trash from the canoe. Now he comes in and volunteers every weekend.

The UEC has shown me that there's more to eating healthy, more to eating than McDonald's. Not that I ate at McDonald's every day. You can have access to your own home-grown food in the city—that was new to me. Working here with nature and seeing educators inspired me to continue being around the Center and learn more.

Since I've gotten involved with the Urban Ecology Center, I appreciate the little things like the sunset and sunrise. Like one morning, I was going to school a couple of months ago, I had an 8:00am communications class. At 7:45, I was walking to class. It was beautiful, spring, I heard all the baby birds, just amazing. I actually put it on Facebook: "You know what? I woke up to a beautiful sunrise, I heard the beautiful chirping of the baby birds, I'm having a good day, I'm having a blessed day, I hope everybody is too." That person wouldn't have been me, before.

I appreciate nature more, being in the parks and teaching people about nature. When we teach someone, we learn something as well. When you're trying to give advice to someone, and you're able to connect the advice to a personal experience, *BAM!*, it connects, and it makes it more important to you and more significant. There are lessons about littering and pollution that become personal.

In summer camp in 2011, we had journal time for kids. I wasn't in charge of that; I was an assistant to an intern. But I tried journaling and thought "Hey, this isn't too bad."

IT WAS MESMERIZING

And during a backpacking trip in the Upper Peninsula of Michigan, I thought, "This is beautiful!" It was mesmerizing, the waterfalls, we found moose tracks, it was really nice. Just having the appreciation of nature, you realize there is so much you can do. You don't always have to go to the mall, you don't always have to go to the movies. You can tie a hammock between two trees and get in and just listen, just relax. I just think that's amazing. It opens up a whole new world.

Especially getting my family into the parks, we've found there are free things that matter. We're an active family—"Let's go for a walk." I think it's cool when I can say "Oh, that's an oriole over there, that's a blue jay, that's a chickadee," just by looking at it or hearing it—just the little things. That's stuff I've learned at the Center by watching educators be so into their work. I feel if someone comes here and they learn just one thing, or they try something new, or they step out of their comfort zone into nature, that's what really matters.

Nature has shaped my life just by seeing the beauty in it and other people's experiences and knowing that I'm the person who can help.

THEY MADE ME WANT TO CARE

If I have a group of campers, I pick up the trash. Or I might say, "Hey, guys, what doesn't belong here? What do you think it is? The soda bottle or the beer bottle!" I learned this from a fellow intern—just keep a plastic bag in your backpack, so if you see litter, pick it up. We're mentoring the kids so if they see that we care, they're going to care as well. And I think that goes back to the educators. They showed me that they cared. They made me want to care. I can pass it on to the kids. That's pretty cool.

Nature wakes you up and makes you aware. You see all the animals being active, you're curious as to how they live their lives, like the squirrels and the chipmunks, the birds and all the insects doing their daily duties. I think it's cool to just sit back and watch. At the Riverside branch of the Urban Ecology Center, they have the beehive. It's just cool to see the bees come and go; the place is kind of like an airport. The bees come in, they come out, they come in, they come out.

ANIMALS HAVE JOBS, LIVES, FAMILIES

There's an analogy between animals and us. They essentially do the same things we do – they have jobs, they have lives, they have families. It makes me want to sit back and think. As far as the morning time, the example I gave you with the bird life… that's a family! They have a house, a mom and dad and kids. I think it's so cool, especially in the morning, everything's so active, especially by the water. I still love going to the beach.

Now I see so much more, and there's a deeper capacity. I was so very blessed that I was able to come back to the Center, because I was an outdoor leader for a year, and then I was a visitor services assistant. I worked as that for a while, temporarily, here at Washington Park. Then I went to college. I came back as a summer education intern. I lead groups of children especially in summer camps. The kids are all different ages. We have everything from three-year-olds with their grandparents or parents, all the way up to teenagers who do overnights. I work with four and five-year-olds in an eco-camp. Those are my favorite groups of kids to work with. And I worked with seven- to eight-year-olds and then five- and six-year-olds.

During winter, I used to ice skate at Red Arrow Park in downtown Milwaukee. The price was nine dollars for each person to rent ice skates. Back when I was an outdoor leader at the UEC, the college membership at the Center was twelve

When I was an education intern at the Urban Ecology Center
(Photo courtesy of Jennifer Johnson)

dollars for a year. So instead of paying nine dollars every time I wanted to skate at Red Arrow, I could go to Washington Park with my twelve-dollar UEC college membership, borrow ice skates for up to two or three days, skate anywhere, bring the skates back, and borrow them many other times. That's only ice skating. That twelve dollars will also let me borrow cross-country skis, snowshoes, sleds, that's only in wintertime. Think about in summertime: kayak, canoe, fishing poles, camping equipment, camping totes you need to make food. It's mind-blowing how many opportunities are here. That's what I tell people.

I really try to get people involved with the Urban Ecology Center. Some kids in my neighborhood are used to being on the block, playing outside with their friends or going to the neighborhood park, but they have never experienced nature in the capacity that the Center supplies. For instance, we have a baby turtle and lots of kids have never seen a baby turtle before. Kids in my neighborhood loved my picture of the baby turtle. Or sometimes if there's some down time and I want to take a kayak, I go out and take a kayak and take some pictures, post them on Facebook, show my family. Kids in the neighbor-hood say, "Oh I want to go on the river." They've never done that before, never been on a boat. But most of them don't know how to swim.

I try to bring them to the Young Scientists club—the oldest girl was like thirteen or so back then—she thought it was totally cool how you could go into the garden, pick vegetables, bring them in here, and make food. I told her, "Yeah, you don't have to have a huge garden to grow a tomato."

THE CENTER ENHANCED ME BEING CONFIDENT

I feel like when you walk into any of the UEC branches, you get the deep feel of nature, the deep feel of the importance of the environment and the things that it supplies. For instance, at Riverside, the furniture is all wood. Everything in that building is recycled. Here at Washington Park, you feel the genuine compassion for the environment and for nature, whether it's by the way we walk, the way we talk, the things we eat, our efforts, like some people eat out of jars, not plastic or Tupperware.

The Center enhanced me being poised and confident. It's such a welcoming place, especially the Washington Park branch. This location works on our mission the best, I think: conducting inner-city families to nature and to experiences they've never had before or may never have had.

We encourage gardening, raising your own crops in the city—and canoeing—lots of people have never done it before—they can be fifty years old or four years old. The staff does its job so well. They'll be walking and identify a plant on the spot. You feel the care, compassion, and love.

I KNOW YOU AND I WILL ALWAYS KNOW YOU

I want to come back next summer. I can't get enough of this place. It's so amazing and the bonds I'm making will be for a lifetime. Take Willie, for example. He's leaving—he's going to Alaska to do something with the Iditarod races. Every time I see him, I get all watery-eyed. But I know that if I need him for anything, anything at all, I can always call or email, and he'll be there if I need him for a reference. It's like, "I know you and I will always know you." If you come back, it will be just like yesterday.

I'm a sophomore at the University of Wisconsin–Stevens Point. I want to be a child-life specialist for children with disabilities or disease. It's like being a social worker, in and out of the hospital. You help children coping with stress, you help with legalities, and so on. I have a communication minor with an emphasis on interpersonal organizational efforts. For instance, I could work with nonprofits that work with families, like the Urban Ecology Center or the Boys and Girls Club.

The UEC influenced my choice of schools. In 2011, I was an outdoor leader. I took a week-long backpack trip through different cities in the state and Michigan's Upper Peninsula. The last stop was the University of Wisconsin Stevens Point. I was so happy we were somewhere with people, somewhere we could take showers—and the Schmeeckle Reserve on campus was cool.

I want there to be more UECs. I like what we're doing in Milwaukee as far as the three different locations, working with schools in a two-mile radius. It's like we're family. I want other cities to experience this, but not if the mission changes, not in a different capacity, not for profit or if it would just be part of a chain. That's one of my fears. Having three really special branches means there's a concentrated number of people who are close, who can bring ideas together and make it even better here. If there started to be a chain of Urban Ecology Centers in different cities, how would that happen? You need everyone on the spectrum to make something work.

Here for instance, our director, Ken Leinbach, can come into any location. He started the Center in a trailer. Just having someone of that power being able to come into a branch is awesome. I've worked for an auto parts store, but it's really different. I've never seen the person walk in who owns or created it, so to me it's just another auto parts store. Not to say it's not special, but it's not special!

I WANT TO MAKE SCIENCE FUN FOR KIDS
Menomonee Valley is the newest branch of the Urban Ecology Center. I feel like it's a UEC, but it needs some time to grow and develop into its own. I get the nature feel and ecological understanding there, but I haven't experienced its own unique feeling when I go in yet. I'm looking forward to that.

I want to make science fun for kids. I want to help them get into the outdoors, I want to help them experience the outdoors and science, instead of being inside a building reading a book about nature. I want kids to get a deeper understanding of nature and science.

I wish that more people would be eco-friendly and realize the importance of nature. Like here at Washington Park, the staff really cares about nature. At orientation, we were talking about stuff at Riverside Park and we were in a particular closet, and someone said, "We're in and out of here, just make sure you turn off the light. This is the only room in the building that doesn't have a sensor." He took a little bit of time out of his whole speech to tell us that. That was cool, you could see that they care about the environment. A lot of people bike to work. You don't see that often. People carpool—it's not just a job for them. You really see that in all aspects of their lives. I wish other people would have some type of understanding to know they can help.

(Photo courtesy of Jennifer Johnson)

Lee Darby, 17 years old at time of interview
(Photo courtesy of Lee Darby)

"The equipment lending program offers a broad array of outdoor rec-reational gear – kayaks, paddleboards, canoes, camping gear, cross-country skis, snowshoes, sleds, skates (at the Washington Park Cen-ter), tennis rackets (for the courts at Riverside Park), lawn games (like croquet and bocce ball), shovels, extension ladders, and more. People sometimes confuse our lending program with a rental program. It's not. It's a free service we offer to our members, because we want to break down all kinds of barriers for people to get outside."
— Ken Leinbach,

Urban Ecology: A Natural Way to Transform
Kids, Parks, Cities, and the World

LEE DARBY:
"LET YOURSELF BE YOUR GUIDE."

THERAPY THROUGH NATURE WAS BETTER THAN THERAPY THROUGH HUMANS

I wasn't a typical kid; I didn't speak until around kindergarten. I was more hands-on than talking. I loved exploring as a child. That compensated for the fact that I couldn't read or talk.

Nature had a good part of changing me. When I was young and had trouble speaking, some part of me felt closer to nature and I felt like I understood it more than some speech therapy that I was going through. Around age two or three, I saw a butterfly, found a book on my own, and learned what the butterfly was. I did it by sight, not by its English name. The book was from back in the 1980s, in a personal collection, *Butterfly Guide of North America*. As much as I remember, it was exciting to me. So, before I knew how to read, I knew twenty-four species of butterflies that I saw in nature and in a book.

Therapy through nature was better than therapy through humans.

I live less than one mile from Washington Park. I'd play in the park and walk the dogs around it. I enjoyed the park.

Before I learned about the Center, I was in nature and then out of nature when I discovered TV—cartoons, news, the *Discovery Channel. Discovery* had nature shows that I liked.

WHEN I FINALLY GOT UPHILL, I ALMOST DID A SONNY BONO

I first started going to the Urban Ecology Center in about 2007, when the Washington Park branch opened. I was walking my two dogs with my parents, and the UEC was having this big party. There was a banner and people outside. I thought that was a good idea.

Everything that I've done at the Center is collected in this one spot in Washington Park, every memory of things I've done here.

I was a "super" volunteer (just a volunteer, but who did a lot more than most)—I tried to be helpful any way I could. I mainly organized a lending closet with hats and gloves. Kids keep them for a day if they need them. We'll never get the stuff clean!

I remember going cross-country skiing for the first time through the Center, at Lapham Peak. I was complaining because I thought it would be easy, but it was a hellish first cross-country ski experience. I had the wrong skis; they were too long for me. Back then I was like five foot, four inches, about 180 centimeters. An intern in a rush situation gave me a 200-centimeter-tall set of skis. The skis had a good wax job; they were really slick racing skis. So, when I was supposed to be going uphill, I couldn't get anywhere for about fifteen minutes. It

Skis at the UEC Riverside Park
(Photo courtesy of the Urban Ecology Center)

was like trying to walk on water. When I finally got uphill, I almost did a Sonny Bono: I bear-hugged a tree, with one leg on each side. It was a dead tree and the tree fell over. After that, I had to walk with my skis. I said, "I'm done with this – this is terrible." But I looked online and found helpful advice about skiing, and realized that intern had screwed up.

In 2014, I became an Urban Ecology Center employee. Now I'm the person who picks out the skis and teaches. I share what I learned online with my students. I do the main rentals, verify the credit cards, check the driver's license, write down the information, take the stuff to your car. I teach cross-country skiing, usually to adults. We take an Urban Ecology Center van and go to Currie Park, the best park in Milwaukee County, in my opinion. In my free time during summer, I go to different parks to see if they would work for skiing.

I lead field trips during spring, summer, and fall, to various parks. I take kids on hikes and help them explore. I point out anything that comes across our path. Of all the parks that I visit as part of my work with the Center, my favorite is Hartung Park in Wauwatosa. It's made from an old quarry and it's an interesting place to be. A lot of planning went into it; it looks nice and there's a good view of Wauwatosa from on top of these massive chunks of limestone on the hill.

Sometimes I go outside at night. You can see and hear things you don't during the day.

I NEVER MET ANYONE WHO DOESN'T LIKE NATURE

I like to let young people find out for themselves what their favorite things are in nature. I tell them, "You don't have to go to Steamboat Springs to find snow. Don't forget about what's close to home. You don't have to go spend money and go far away."

I never met anyone who doesn't like nature. I tell them, "Nature has everything you're interested in." Not everybody likes everything. I tell them, "Go to Riverside Park first. If you like it, then you can try other parks. Let yourself be your guide. What they have there is for you to discover."

NATURE CAN TAKE AWAY STRESS

I see many young people stressed out. They just don't go outside. Nature can take away stress from people young and old. When I tell that to young people, they get more calm.

DON'T RUN AWAY FROM LIFE; FACE IT HEAD ON

I'm in a two-year paid internship at the Urban Ecology Center where I am an outdoor leader. I'm on the final year of the internship, but my life with the UEC is not done. I have successfully mentored the next group of outdoor leaders. I want to do an internship, then be an environmental educator at the Center.

I'm a junior at Pius High School. I want to go to college for environmental research or natural sciences (biology, ecology) either at the University of Wisconsin-Stevens Point, Macalester College, or the University of Minnesota-Twin Cities.

My wish for the Urban Ecology Center is that it should expand in the communities it's already serving. It could offer more to the community, like I've seen a lot of non-profits that lead extended trips in Northern Wisconsin and Michigan. I think we should try to use that idea, but put our own twist on it. The UEC could lead extended trips, like for a whole week, maybe in town, maybe farther away—tailored camping trips.

My wish for the world is to not forget about nature because I think we can do something. We forget about common sense and things we've already been taught. Don't run away from life; face it head on. Life will be better than we are trying to make it be.

PS AUGUST 2016

A lot has changed since I gave this interview. I've expanded my interest into photography. I now operate numerous social media accounts dedicated to a new interest of mine: exploring abandoned buildings. I am considering other jobs now that I have completed my internship at the UEC. I have expanded my interest in visual art, and am making two professional art portfolios with upwards of forty pieces in each.

*Night sledding at Mitchell Park, UEC Young Scientists Club
(Photo courtesy of the Urban Ecology Center)*

Daniel Rawley, 20 years old at time of interview
(Photo courtesy of the Urban Ecology Center, Washington Park)

"I don't know anyone who has worked at the Urban Ecology Center who has not been changed in some way by it, be they a volunteer or an employee."
—Ken Leinbach,
Urban Ecology: A Natural Way to Transform
Kids, Parks, Cities, and the World

Daniel Rawley: "Kindness ensues."

I'd come out with toads or worms

The love of nature had to have been in me. My first word, and it wasn't even a word, was—I would watch the crows outside my window and I would say, "Caw." It was always instilled in me that I was "nature boy." My family would call me that, and my friends. And it was true, because whenever we were in a place, like my brother's baseball games, everyone would be like, "Where's Daniel?" and I would be in the woods and I'd come out with toads or worms.

My siblings don't love nature as much as I do. They're kind of sports nuts, like city folk. I've grown up in Milwaukee my whole life, on a regular city lot, not in the suburbs. What I love so much about the Urban Ecology Center is that they are focused on green space in urban areas and providing access to a vibrant healthy green space to community members to come appreciate it.

Falling in the river with all my clothes on

My first experience at the Urban Ecology Center was when they first built their new building in Riverside Park. I was about eleven or twelve. I don't know if it was a turning point for me; it was a summer camp. I don't know if I could have recited "Urban Ecology Center" after going there. I had a really good time and learned a lot of new things. We mixed mustard powder with water and put it in the soil and we watched worms come up from the soil because it irritated them so much. I thought that was the coolest thing. I remember falling in the river, kayaking, with all my clothes on. I fell by accident and then I convinced a lot of other people in the group to also jump in. I don't think it was the best idea because it wasn't the cleanest river.

I remember swimming in Lake Michigan. We took a trip to I think it must have been a UEC supporter's house who lives on Lake Michigan. It was a very cold, overcast day. Lake Michigan was even colder. There were very slippery rocks, not a sandy beach by any means. We stayed in the water most of the day— we were kids.

I don't remember why I didn't come back every year. I was probably getting too old for the summer camps. I came back my sophomore year of high school for the outdoor leader program. My best friend's mom was talking to this man, he had a huge beard and long hair, and he recommended the outdoor leader program to her son, who was my age. She was like, "That's not for my son," and she immediately thought of me and called me and explained it. I applied and then got to know that man who she had talked to.

IT SOUNDED LIKE THE COOLEST JOB

I applied because my whole entire life has pretty much been focused on nature and loving nature and doing things in nature

—so when I saw that there was a position for someone as young as me to be able to teach kids and work at the UEC, it sounded like the coolest job in the whole entire world. The experience was very exciting. I was probably fifteen, or just sixteen. It really was the coolest job I've ever had.

MY MOM WAS TERRIFIED

After my summer training in Outdoor Leaders, I got assigned to Washington Park branch and stayed here for a little over two years, until I left for college, because I loved it so much.

That's me on the far right, clowning around in the UEC Washington Park with two outdoor leaders. (Photo courtesy of the Urban Ecology Center)

I found my niche in the animal room. They're all my favorites. I think the cutest and least-appreciated is Gilbert the American toad. Me and him, we go way back. I used to do outreach where I'd take animals to schools and teach to kindergartners. I would take all the animals with me to my house and leave from my house to the school in the morning so I wouldn't have to go to the Center first. I'd take them in little portable travel tanks. Then I'd have sleepovers with all my favorite animals.

Foxy the fox snake would be crawling around my room, like on the crown molding. She was such a good climber. My mom was terrified and would not come in my room. Finally, I just wouldn't point him out to her. One time, Gilbert the toad got sick before I took him. He was kind of green and slimy-looking and he was shedding his skin—you know, they peel it all off and then they eat it. He choked on his skin and couldn't swallow it down so I pulled it out of his mouth—it was like a clown trick. He made it, though. I hope he's still there, still alive.

My favorite appeal with Gilbert, when I was teaching a class, was I'd ask the kids, "Do you want to say hi to Gilbert? He'll say hi back."

He's a boy toad, so I'd pick him up from his stomach and then he starts peeping, he chirps when you pick him up just right. The reason for that is if another male tries to mount him, he pretty much yells at him: "Hey, man, this is not going to work out. Back off." That's how you can tell male and female toads apart.

This trick quiets kids down, too. I tell them, "You have to be really quiet to hear him say 'hi.'"

Mostly I visited Lincoln Elementary in Wauwatosa—they have a special day where people come in to teach, the last thing, for an hour.

WE LIVED LIKE KINGS ON THE RIVER

During my last summer with the outdoor leader program at the Urban Ecology Center, they were looking for a new trip. All the outdoor leaders get to go on a trip. There was one in the Grand Canyon, a rafting trip, and they sent me alone on a plane to review this program, eight days rafting down the Colorado River through the Grand Canyon. Afterwards, I gave my opinion and feedback about the trip itself.

It was awesome, one of the greatest experiences of my life, as you could imagine. We lived like kings on the river. They brought so much food; we had a Thanksgiving dinner, barbeque, they fit so much on those rubber rafts. We did a lot of floating but there were also some huge, very memorable rapids. And the water was freezing.

The organization we went through is Grand Canyon Youth and they send a lot of kids down on scholarships. I didn't have to do any of this, but from what I heard, the kids had to raise a lot of the money themselves through fundraisers and do a lot of community work to get to be able to go down there. I came into it not really knowing anything about it, just "I'm going on a trip."

THEY LET KIDS LEAD

I built that really big fish tank at the Washington Park Center. It was definitely my longest-running project at the UEC. There's a philanthropist organization in Milwaukee called "Lead to Change." They're run by a majority of youth, like 51 percent. They have a budget and they fund different projects in the Milwaukee area. Every year they give out two five thousand dollar grants. I wrote a grant for the community aquarium—the plan was just a giant fish tank with native species.

Then I gathered a bunch of the kids who were regulars, good kids with cute faces, and we gave the Lead to Change board a presentation and drew a giant fish tank on paper so they could get an idea of how big it was going to be and had the kids give reasons why we should be funded for this project. It was cool. I wrote the grant and the kids helped with the presentation to the board. I was seventeen probably. That's why I like the Urban Ecology Center: they gave me so many opportunities, they let kids lead.

We had a lot of fish already, and the branch manager here and I got to know the curator of the Milwaukee County Zoo, who runs the aquarium there, and we had given him some fish. We gave him a bass that was really mean so he could put it in his tank. Then he gave us some small fish we could raise and put in the new giant tank. It's all Wisconsin native fish. It took a long time. We got the money and a year later all we had to show for it was a fish tank stand. Ideas were always coming up in my head: designing the filtration for it, how it's going to work on the inside. What held the project up is we had to build a whole new animal room for it because it was so big it wouldn't fit into our other one. We didn't own that part of the building.

So, the greatest part about it is that it really got the ball rolling to expand. That new entranceway with the animal room and the fish tank – that's not how it was before. It's been a snowball effect, real positive change, just from fish.

IT WAS FUN TO TEACH ADULTS SOMETHING NEW

It's crazy how much nature is right here in the city, at Washington Park. I love birds and bird watching. I think with the Department of Natural Resources, we had installed a sonar receptor thing, on the roof here, that collected bat calls and bird calls and they told us that we had the second most diverse population of birds and bats on the Lake Michigan coast. It's a green space so when birds are migrating over, they see that big patch of green in the middle of the city.

One of my favorite things to teach was the water safety course with canoeing every Saturday. The class was full of adults. They weren't always complete rookies, but the thing is at the Urban Ecology Center, you have to be a member to take out a canoe, and you have to take the water safety course. So, I was the one who would explain the different paddle strokes and the safety things, how to put on life vests. It was fun being able to teach adults something new. I was only seventeen years old.

What I always loved about teaching, what I still love about teaching, is I love animals and I love holding animals, and I feel like I'm the best educator when I'm holding an animal. My usual approach is to be a little over the top excited and enthusiastic – I think the place where kids get the most excited is when there's an example there, like you're looking at a tree or I'm holding a snake or something. Then you really get the kids' attention and then you see that look in their eyes. They get so excited about the snake you have in your hands and they get to touch it for the first time. They learn that snakes are not slimy, and they're not scary god-awful creatures, that they're something to marvel at, to appreciate.

Now, during summer break, I'm working for the County Parks, the Forestry Department. Forestry does a lot of things; I just do playgrounds. I drive around with my partner to different playgrounds and maintain them and clean them up. It's nice, we're in charge of all 120 playgrounds, just us two. We get to see every park, and Milwaukee has a lot of beautiful parks. I didn't even realize how many. Washington Park has like five little tiny playgrounds. There are some parks without playgrounds. There are definitely over 100 parks. We pick up litter, make sure equipment is safe. We encounter kids. My partner really doesn't like it when I talk or play with the kids, because he thinks it's a liability. He keeps to himself. But when I'm sweeping off leaves, all the kids want to help sweep with me, and then of course, I teach them what tree the leaves came from. They're usually interested. I have them repeat it when I'm leaving.

One little girl gave me a gift—it was leaves. She said, "Here I want you to have this."

I asked her, "What kind of leaves are they?"

She said, "Oak."

I said, "Yes, very good." So, I'm just trying to get my little fill of outdoor education in.

When I'm cleaning the parks and I see litter, I just want to scream…there are so many communities that don't appreciate the awesome parks that we have. At the playgrounds, I can't believe the amount of graffiti I have to remove, and vandalism I see. The playground here at Washington Park has been lit on fire like five times this summer. The shenanigans some people get into when the Urban Ecology Center is right here as an outlet!

Last summer, I worked at Holiday Home Camp. It was a little more interesting than my work with the playgrounds this summer. Holiday Home Camp is a summer camp on Lake Geneva, Wisconsin. It's the oldest summer camp in the United States that is still in its original location and still using its original building, over 125 years old.

The camp was founded by factory owners in Chicago who wanted someplace for their workers to bring their kids and have a vacation and get fresh air. It was during the fresh air movement. They thought you needed a daily dose of fresh air. It was in the 1800s—during that time, they built a lot of screen porches on houses—all part of the fresh air movement. So, the camp has pretty much been founded on the same principle and now what we do is we pick up kids from the inner city of Milwaukee, Racine, mostly Chicago, and bring them there, usually for free. I was the environmental educator. I had a tiny nature shack with a few turtles and snakes, a ton of bird feathers that kids would give me.

Nature does so much for kids. I just look at what it's done for me—opened up so many doors and it makes you a more well-rounded person. You want to learn and appreciate, it makes you kind, more smart, it makes you a more peaceful, relaxed, calm person—not constantly focusing on traffic, more like, "Oh, look at that tree."

It's stewardship, caring for something that you see so many people treating poorly—caring for the earth—it's selfless, kind. Community comes together – like what the Urban Ecology Center does – community comes together for that one goal, to be good to the earth, to be stewards of the earth, and kindness ensues.

I'm a vegetarian for so many different reasons. I like to be a sustainable citizen of the earth. I feel right now with the number of people we have and the way we get a lot of our food, vegetarianism is the easiest way for me to make a small impact. It's not hard for me to give up meat. And if it's something I can do, why not do it? And I ride my bike everywhere. I don't own a car. I don't have plans to own a car, unless I really need one.

IT DOES GIVE YOU EVERYTHING

I'm going to be a junior at the University of Wisconsin–Stevens Point. I'm studying water resources; I like water. When I came fresh from the UEC and high school, I was going for wildlife education; that's kind of what I was doing at the Center. I definitely saw myself doing that in the future. And then I thought it wasn't very practical. Stevens Point turns out a lot of wildlife students, kind of saturates it. I think that it's still something I'm capable of doing with any sort of natural resource degree. People who work here, like Erick (page 142), went for chemistry. So, it's still possible.

I wish for the UEC to keep doing the good that they're doing. They've been progressing, they just built a new center, the community has really gotten behind them. I hope that Milwaukee continues to support such a good thing. The UEC has been recognized nationally. Places I go to and say that I worked at the Center – people are familiar with it. I've heard it in Arizona, a lot of people in Stevens Point – they'll say "I've been to the UEC a few times," and I'll say, "I worked there."

I'd like people to have a strong appreciation for the environment and nature, and a respect for it because it does give you everything and people just take and take and take – we just can't do that forever, it's just not going to work out in our favor. It's a group mentality about it—it's got to be a social change.

Terrance Davis, 34 years old at time of interview

"Leading a community center is different from leading a company or a profit-motivated business. Leading a community center is all about finding and facilitating the passion and skills of those around you, and then stepping away to let them shine. It's about building a container, so to speak—meaning the organization as a whole—that maximizes their joy, their work styles, and their productivity."
—Ken Leinbach,
*Urban Ecology: A Natural Way to Transform
Kids, Parks, Cities, and the World*

Terrance Davis:
"It's Brought Us Closer"

My dad taught me how to wield an axe

I had a connection to nature when I was growing up. I did quite a lot of fishing with my dad. We lived in Milwaukee and we fished in Lake Michigan or Big Muskego and Little Muskego Lakes. My dad also taught me how to wield an axe. We had a real fireplace. Sometimes we bought firewood but other times we cut deadwood from the trees in our backyard or in parks.

I'm a multitasker—I can mop and learn

I'm the visitor services specialist at the Urban Ecology Center Washington Park branch. I started out in maintenance in March of 2012.

When I first started, I was at the Riverside location and I found out there was a location at Washington Park. I grew up in that neighborhood, so I requested to be transferred there.

I'm a multi-tasker—I can mop and learn. While I was picking up trash in the park, I saw lots of people I knew from back then who now have kids, so I began to talk to them about UEC programs. That brought people in. A lot of them became members, joined programs like the Young Scientists club, went to maple sugaring.

It was noticed. People mentioned me, how they were referred by me to the Center. Around May of 2013, I was offered an official position of visitor services assistant. I would lend equipment, engage people, encourage membership. Now I also order equipment, keep inventory, and make reports for funding.

I got the job at the Urban Ecology Center through a transitional job program that was through the YWCA. I had some good jobs in the past, but I was having trouble finding one around 2011. I'm truly grateful for everything the UEC offers me and for everything I can offer the Center. I'm so grateful that my kids can participate in the programs.

WHEN YOU LIKE NATURE, YOU HAVE MORE THINGS TO DO

Before, I couldn't identify a bird species. Now I know the sounds of birds. I've become environmentally aware, for example about my energy use, about monarch eggs on milkweed. There are so many small facts to be able to tell my kids. They're more interested in nature, they can identify species, they like canoeing. They're girls, seven and eight years old. They've gone to Urban Ecology Center summer camp and the Young Scientists club.

We have two great blue herons that hang around the lagoon at Washington Park. We also have black-crowned herons and little green herons, but we don't see them as often —they're smaller and not that visible. I couldn't even have told you about these birds a couple of years ago, before I got involved at the Center. Enjoying nature just makes life more enjoyable. They say "Variety is the spice... ." When you like nature, you have more things to do. You can get involved. Life has more flavor.

If people have a connection to nature when they're young, they will help steward the land in some way when they're older. Being environmentally aware promotes a healthier lifestyle. I find myself eating differently. I still like fried chicken, but I'll eat peanut butter on celery, or quinoa.

I plant a garden with my children, on raised garden beds. It's brought us closer; it's a whole other way to bond. When we're gardening, we might talk about our favorite vegetables or fruits. But a lot of times what we talk about has nothing to do with gardening. Gardening gave us the opportunity to talk about stuff we usually don't have the time to talk about. The girls can tell me about things I do that they appreciate or that they don't appreciate. I can talk to them about things they do that make me proud, like getting good grades or helping out with housework. Besides gardening, we sometimes go skating or biking.

IN THE FUTURE, THE COMMUNITY CAN PICK THE FRUIT

I want to stay with the UEC. I like to be on site, ready to listen to others, ready to put my two cents in. I think kids feel welcomed by me because I'm friendly. I tell my peers about the Center; sometimes I feel I'm a bit excessive talking about it. I have grown passionate about it. The culture here, it's a happy-go-lucky environment. I'm always smiling. I like to share what I learn and work on learning more.

The volunteers and volunteer coordinators are land stewards. They're people who keep this place looking beautiful. The volunteers and employees get rid of invasive plants, for example. I always hear people saying, "The park is so beautiful." We have an orchard organized, with apples and more. This is a project we've made happen with the help of volunteers. They're now baby trees, but in the future, the community can pick the fruit.

I hope everybody can get the message that the Urban Ecology Center has, to promote and protect the land, not destroy it. I want to learn as much as I can and grow as much as I can. I'm now completely comfortable with the decisions I make for my family.

My wish for our world is that people will get out and enjoy nature. I want everybody to be aware so my children's great-grandchildren have a place to be connected to nature.

PS—October 2016

This summer we harvested fruit from trees that we planted in Washington Park. The orchard is located on the northeast corner of the park, on the corner of Lisbon Road and 40th Street. Any neighbor can come and pick the fruit. I've seen them doing it. They don't really say anything; they're chewing!

First, we harvested cherries, then peaches, then apples. The cherry harvest came about the time that Michelle Obama presented Milwaukee with an award for getting children outdoors.

For the cherry harvest, there was a big group of children from the Boys and Girls Club and the YWCA. They picked the cherries and ate them. The mayor was here, and the TV news, and a representative from the YMCA. One of our outdoor leaders spoke.

The kids who did the harvest also put in some plants that will help the soil so the trees bear fruit next year.

Menomonee Valley Urban Ecology Center building and grounds
(Photo courtesy of Sarina Counard-Ryals)

"When I began this work two decades ago, the Oak Leaf Trail, a bicycle commuter trail that runs through Riverside Park, was rarely used because it was perceived to be unsafe. ... All the activity we provide along that trail, as well as what we do to help provide a safe haven in what was one of the most unsafe stretches of the Trail, have had a major impact on the safety of the area, and thus on the neighborhood, the community, and the environment. "

—Ken Leinbach,
Urban Ecology: A Natural Way to Transform
Kids, Parks, Cities, and the World

PART 4

MENOMONEE VALLEY STAFF

Glenna Holstein, 28 years old at time of interview
Glenna at the Grand Opening of Three Bridges Park, 2013.
(Photo courtesy of Eddee Daniel)

*"I can't stress enough the importance of involving and bringing
people along with a vision, such that they feel ownership, too."*
—Ken Leinbach,
*Urban Ecology: A Natural Way to Transform
Kids, Parks, Cities, and the World*

GLENNA HOLSTEIN:
"HUMANS AND GREEN THINGS"

A DOUBLE-WIDE TRAILER STARTS IT ALL

I guess I was always kind of a nature kid. I grew up about one mile north of Riverside Park, really close to Cambridge Woods. I was always playing in the woods, scampering around in there. In fact, I think I probably had trouble making friends as a kid because my parents were much more encouraging of me playing out in the woods than most parents were. I would want

The original Urban Ecology Trailer at Riverside Park
(Photo courtesy of the Urban Ecology Center)

Me swinging on a vine in 1994
(Photo courtesy of Suzy Holstein)

to go play in the woods and other people's parents wouldn't let them, so I played a lot by myself, but a lot in the woods. So—a lot of imagination, a lot of throwing rocks, a lot of trying to build swings in trees and things like that, with varying degrees of success.

I don't remember when the Urban Ecology Center first became part of my life. My mom says we went to programs there when I was a kid. I don't remember that, but I do remember when I was in high school, I started to get very interested in environmental issues. I remember wanting to get involved in volunteering—so a couple of friends from my high school and I went to volunteer and I kind of never left since then, really.

Me, age 9, looking at the Grand Canyon
(Photo courtesy of Suzy Holstein)

IT WAS SORT OF MAGICAL IN THERE

The UEC at that time was a little double-wide trailer in the back corner of Riverside High School campus, which was about a mile from my school, Shorewood High School. I think about walking into the little trailer—it's amazing to me how special that place always has been—it never has needed the bells and whistles of a fancy building. Everyone there just exuded the passion for something really important and really local. I remember feeling like I had found my place in a powerful way…and I couldn't even tell you what it was because if you look at pictures of the trailer at that time, you wouldn't think it was anything special. Half of it was humans and half of it was animals in tanks. But it was sort of magical in there.

It was so exciting to be part of that work even in a volunteer role. I don't even remember what we did the first time we went there, but I remember continually feeling this gravitational pull toward the work that was being done there and toward the really positive attitude that the Center takes toward environmental issues. It can be very depressing to think about the

Me back at the Grand Canyon in 2015
(Photo courtesy of Lauren Boyd)

environmental crises of our times, and at the UEC it was always positive, it was always focused on what you could do and how much fun it was to be outside. That's so important; that's what kept pulling me back and what pulls a lot of people back I think.

I took an amazing course in high school that was focused on environmental stewardship of the Milwaukee River watershed. We biked and hiked to the headwaters of the Milwaukee River, then canoed all the way down the river, all the while reading things like Aldo Leopold and discussing them. Each of us got little facts about different natural elements we might encounter; whenever we saw them, we had to stop and tell who we were with about them. My topic was ephemeral ponds, which are ponds that dry up during certain times of year.

Sometimes there are tadpoles and baby salamanders in them. When I first saw an ephemeral pond, I was so excited because I knew what it was and I could tell other people.

I THINK I WAS TOO SMALL FOR THE BIKE

I volunteered at the Urban Ecology Center in high school and had an internship there in college. I was at the UEC two summers. The first summer was a volunteer internship. It was the year we were moving into the new building. I did all sorts of weird stuff that year: scrubbing graffiti off the playground, weed whacking, database work, going to get items people were donating.

People are so generous to the Center, but there was not that much space in the trailer for all the things people had been hanging onto, stuff they had wanted to give us for a long time, like ponytail palm trees or a tandem bike, that was a fun one. We thought we could ride it back, but it didn't work as well as we had intended; I think I was too small for the bike.

IT'S NOT THE BUILDING;
IT'S THE MEANINGFUL WORK

So, that first summer I was doing whatever was needed, and helping to plan the volunteer celebration for the soft opening of the building. That was really neat, to be one of the first people in the new Riverside Park building. It's really a magnificent building, and a little bit undiscovered. I love seeing people discovering the UEC. I see them walk in and I see their eyes light up, like "I had no idea this was here" – and I'm always a little envious because I don't remember exactly that moment for myself, but I know it was in the trailer.

The Riverside Park building is so impressive but I don't even think that's what people are feeling when they walk in, because I felt it in the trailer, you know. It's not the building; it's the meaningful work being done and the attitude of compassion and excitement around building a better ecological and human community. You feel that when you walk into any of our three centers now—I certainly felt it when I walked into the trailer.

The second summer, I was a paid intern and I worked with summer camps, so that was my first hands-on experience with environmental education. I got to work with some phenomenal educators, some who are still at the Center, and some who have moved on to do other wonderful and amazing things.

I was getting paid to play outside with kids, and I thought, "Wow, this could be a job. That's cool."

I don't know if I had this awareness at that time, but developed it since then, that it's becoming more and more difficult for kids to play outside. Not only are parents more nervous about it, for lots of very legitimate reasons, but I found kids don't know how. They've got a lot of prescribed play and prescribed activities in their lives, so getting to teach kids how to play outside is kind of a cool job. I sort of wish it wasn't one that was necessary. But if someone's got to do it, sign me up.

"WELL? YOU WANT TO DO SOMETHING?"

I first volunteered at the Urban Ecology Center with a couple of friends who were in the Global Action Environmental Group at my high school. The first year I had the internship, another friend from high school also had one; we didn't coordinate that but we were both there. It's funny because now I'd say that all my friends do things at the UEC. That goes two directions: one direction is that I tell everyone I know about the Center and make them come to things; the other is that many of my friends now are people who work at the Center, my colleagues. My colleagues are some of the most amazing people I know, and the fact that I get to come to work with them every day makes it pretty easy to do.

Everybody here is just so darn nice. Several of us who work here live close to each other and we're together all week and have a great time, and there are many times when the weekend comes and we're like, "Well? You want to do something?"

The people that the UEC attracts as staff and volunteers and our community in general are incredible people. They have that positive outlook on what the solutions are for environmental problems and social problems too. Most of what we do as the solution is building positive community. It's great to work at a place that values building positive community, because then you have this great community you work in. It's a circle.

THE UEC AND MILWAUKEE
HAVE A GRAVITATIONAL PULL

Because of my work at the Center and that amazing watershed class in high school, as well as many other complementary experiences, I decided that I wanted to study environmental something-or-other. I went to school at Pomona College in Southern California for Environmental Analysis. The track (of the Environmental Analysis major) that I did was "Race, Class, Gender, and the Environment," which focused on the intersection between social and human issues and environmental issues. Really you can't pull them apart. I think a lot of times we try to, but that intersection is where my passion is, so I wanted to learn more about it. During that time, I also discovered teaching is really compelling to me.

Los Angeles is an interesting place to study environmental issues. It's a beautiful place full of interesting, wonderful people, but not a place that a girl who grew up around water wants to be. In my first semester, I felt a little off for the first few weeks. I wandered around one day and wound up at a botanic garden and stumbled upon a little retention pond. There were some turtles. I felt so good. I realized I hadn't lived anywhere without water everywhere before, so finding that pond was like, "Oh, I miss water – that's why I feel so strange!" That gave me an understanding of how your environment can shape your personality, your sense of place. That was an interesting realization, and I got drawn back to the water.

I lived in Albuquerque, New Mexico for a while. (The Rio Grande River runs through it, so there was water for me!) I got to teach environmental education there for a year, which was an incredible experience, a fun job. It was exciting to get to know a new place, and also illustrated to me how much of a Milwaukee girl I really am. I mean I love Albuquerque, and could see myself going back there someday possibly, but like I say, the Urban Ecology Center and Milwaukee kind of have a gravitational pull for me. I'm happy to be back here.

In Los Angeles, I did some tutoring in classrooms, and teaching day laborers who were just learning English. I could see the sense of empowerment in people as they were learning —it made me want to teach. So, I initially went into teaching in a classroom. I taught second grade in a bilingual classroom in Chicago. Not surprisingly, I loved teaching kids but didn't like being inside all day. Probably anyone who knew me could have told you that would have happened, but sometimes you have to figure these things out yourself. So right as I was figuring that out, the Urban Ecology Center posted an environmental educator position. The rest is history.

I think I knew in high school that the UEC was a place I'd like to work someday if I could, so it hit the nail on the head with the dream job. It was impressive to me that life worked out that way; it was pretty amazing. What's so incredible is that was my dream job at the time, and working at the Center has only become more my dream job as I've learned more about it and been able to do more things at work. So, I've gotten my dream job more than once.

THERE IS NO "TYPICAL DAY"

Early on in my work at the Center, I would describe my job as environmental education. Working now as branch manager is very wide-ranging, so it's a little harder to describe. There is no "typical day." I've struggled to try to capture what my job is. A lot of my role is creating space or creating place. That can be for the staff who work here, creating space for the ideas they have and a place for them to spring off from to bring those ideas to life.

It's also about creating a space where people in the surrounding neighborhood feel invited to ecological literacy, to play outside, to be part of a community; that's a big part of my work. That means working with staff, with folks in my neighborhood, with other organizations that are active in this community, and with the city and state to create the outdoor space. That's a critical part of what we are—this is our outdoor classroom. My job is helping to shape that as well.

When I try to be succinct about what my job is, it really comes down to working with people to create space. It's not anything I could do on my own, or would want to do on my own. It's a collaborative effort. A lot of times I get to be the connection piece: I help people figure out what they need to solve the problem they're working on, or help make the idea they have come to life. That's a really exciting place to be because it's a lot like teaching in many ways. I get to see what people want to accomplish or learn, and help empower them to make it real. It could be a visitor, a staff person, an organization in the community that's looking for a way to make something happen.

And I still get to teach sometimes. This week I'm teaching an Early Adventurers' Camp. That's one where three- and four-year-olds come with their parents, and we go on mini-excursions and do puppet shows and make crafts that look like little animals—all helping kids and their parents play outside.

EVERYBODY'S A MENTOR

Parents are the primary mentors for their kids. So, if they can learn a little something, that's so much of what the UEC does; it's mentorship. That's also my story – one of mentorship. There are so many people at the UEC who helped me grow into an environmental educator and into my job here. Beyond that, they helped me grow into a place where I feel at home and feel like I have the capacity and desire to look outward and make things better.

I credit a lot of folks at the Center with mentoring me into that. The exciting thing about transitioning from educator to branch manager is that I feel like I got to receive so much from the UEC and now I can start giving that back, being a mentor, as scary as that sounds sometimes. That's the cool thing about the Urban Ecology Center: everybody's a mentor. The little kids mentor the littler kids and sometimes they mentor the adults, too. Kids often see things that adults don't see. Mentorship goes both ways. That's something that's really important here.

I DIDN'T WANT TO YELL AT THEM

In July 2012, before we opened the Menomonee Valley Center, we had an artist working on a mosaic with the community, in the building. We had open hours that people could work.

One afternoon, I looked out the window and noticed a group of kids gathering on the bike path. I had seen them around often and was curious as to what they were up to. As I watched, it became clear that they were carefully laying rocks across the path, apparently hoping that some hapless biker would be amusingly upended by their construction.

I was unsure what to do. I didn't want to yell at them—they are the reason we are here, after all. But I couldn't ignore them either. So, I went outside, introduced myself, told them about the Center and the community mosaic project that was happening in preparation for the Grand Opening, and said "You know, for the mosaic, we thought it would be cool to have rocks incorporated in the design. Since you guys have conveniently collected a bunch of rocks, would you mind bringing them inside and donating them to the project?"

And, I kid you not, those teenage boys picked up as many rocks as they could carry (even filled their pockets!) and brought them inside with me.

And as soon as they were in, I saw that "This is real?" look come over their faces. I showed them the slide, the overlook, the future animal room, and they were hooked!

"Come back tomorrow!" I said as they left smiling. I added, "You can help with the mosaic!"

And they did! One of them, Marcel, has come back nearly every day to help with the mosaic and has even come to a

Volunteer Orientation. In fact, he was recently overheard telling some of his friends, "Yeah, this is the Urban Ecology Center...I pretty much work here!"

THE BIGGEST BARRIER TO PLAYING OUTSIDE IS FEAR

There are so many reasons to be outside. It's always important to understand the community you're part of. People struggle a lot understanding "place" in a globalized flat world. They feel lost in the big world. Being outside and having a comfort with nature nearby and a sense of place and belonging, feeling they're part of this organism—it's so healing, calming, important.

In a community health assessment project with the Medical College of Wisconsin, we asked how often children play outside and how they felt. So many recognized that they felt calmer and happier outside. The biggest barrier to playing outside is fear.

Kids don't ask why they should play outside; they ask how. They ask, "What can we do here?"

We show them that they can find snakes, look for inverte-brates, make bergamot tea. Especially for kids in a distressful situation, their world looks small; they feel trapped. When they go outside, they get a glimpse of something bigger. It can open their world and let light in.

This is my story, too. It's not coincidental that I love Milwau-kee as much as I do. It's largely because of my ecological understanding of this place. In nature, you see something beyond your idea of the world.

THAT DAY IT TURNED FROM A PROJECT TO A PARK

My favorite thing that I ever did with the Urban Ecology Center happened exactly a year ago. We opened Three Bridges Park. That was an incredible day. We worked with so many different people to build the park, and we wanted to create a celebration that was reflective of what we hoped the park would be. We hoped that it would be a gathering place where people from all different neighborhoods, backgrounds, and interests would come together and take ownership of this park.

We invited many different people to take part in the celebration. The neighborhood is full of creative and generous people. Nearly a thousand people showed up to celebrate. We processed from all three entrances of the park with drummers, and came together at the center of the park at 33rd Court, where there's a platform. The park is at a crossroads of many different neighborhoods. We had groups from some of the schools we work with.

The community organizations brought folks from their different groups to the entrances that were closest to their neighborhood. It was really neat to have representatives from some of our schools coming in this way, and the 16th Street Community Health Center coming in this way, and Journey House and some of the other major players in this neighbor-hood bringing folks to march in and show "It's open and we're using it and we're all coming in together."

We had a *Baile Folklorico*, martial arts, hula-hoops, face painting, people trying out kayaks, all these ways I might have never thought of to use a park. Opening it up to the creativity of so many people was a beautiful illustration of how much people love green space and will figure out a way to use it.

Me enjoying autumn in a tree, Riverside Park 2011
(Photo courtesy of John Suhar)

That day it turned from a project into a park. It was so exciting. People took it and ran and started using it.

THE CENTER IS SO DIFFERENT FOR EVERYBODY

The Center is so different for everybody. One of the things I value so much about the UEC is that we try to meet people where they are. For some people, their favorite thing might be a birding trip where we go and identify birds; it's very biologically focused, something where their ecological literacy is pretty high to begin with, and they do this adventure that pushes their learning.

For other people, their favorite thing might be walking through the park, or taking a cooking class, or knowing there's a place where somebody will listen to their ideas. It's not the same for each person and we're very intentional about trying to be diverse in our approach, in our programming so that we can be a meaningful place for people who have different interests and different access points.

THERE'S A LOT OF WORK TO DO

Doing this job, there's a variety of things and ways I get to interact with places and people. This is part of why I love Milwaukee—for me, it's all about humans and green things. There's a lot of work to do. I want to keep working as long as there's work to do.

The Urban Ecology Center has grown a lot in the last five years. I wish for the Center to grow in the way we are able to affect people and effect change in how different communities relate to nature. My hope is that this is not growth that takes us away from what I felt walking into that tiny trailer. Bigger can be scary. What makes us unique is our intention and our appreciation for the individual and the community. I hope that can stay the same in the future.

My wish for our world is that everyone can either find or create a place where they feel a connection to their community, ecological and human. My wish is for us as a species to work at creating a place where people feel they're part of a community, that they feel valued and responsible to their community.

Maple sugaring at Washington Park
(Photo courtesy of Taylor Chobanian)

Great Blue Heron
(Photo courtesy of Matt Flower)

GLOSSARY
&
RECOMMENDED READING

Cedar Waxwing
(Photo courtesy of Matt Flower)

GLOSSARY

Aldo Leopold – born in Wisconsin, an American author, naturalist, philosopher, scientist, forester, conservationist, and environmentalist (1887–1948).

algae – a type of organism, usually aquatic, distinguished from plants by the absence of true roots, stems, and leaves. You may see green algae growth in a home aquarium or on a lake during hot weather.

aquaponics – any system that combines conventional aqua-culture (raising aquatic animals such as snails, fish, or crayfish in tanks) with hydroponics (cultivating plants in water) in a symbiotic environment.

aquatic – living or growing in water.

arboretum – a plot of land on which many different trees or shrubs are grown for study or display.

aromatic - having a pleasant smell.

bachelor's degree – a certification awarded by a college or university to a person who has completed studies for gradua-tion.

bass – a fish common to Wisconsin lakes.

belayer – a person who controls the safety rope for another person who is climbing.

bergamot – an aromatic wildflower.

biodiversity – a wide variety of plant and animal species in an environment.

bio-phobia – fear of living things.

bird banding – a process of affixing small "bracelets" onto the legs of captured birds before releasing them, for the purpose of identifying their age, gender, and origin on later capture dates.

birder – a person who enjoys watching, listening to, and identifying birds.

birding – also known as "bird-watching" – the process of watching for, listening to, and identifying birds.

bird surveys – a scientific accounting of species of birds in a specific environment at a specific time.

bird walk – a walk in nature for the purpose of enjoying the signs, sights, and sounds of birds.

blue jay – a common crested bird with a bright blue back and a grey breast.

bluff – a land formation with a bold and nearly perpendicular front, often along a coastline.

botanic garden – a garden for the exhibition and scientific study of collected, growing plants, usually in association with greenhouses, herbariums, laboratories, etc.

breeding – the producing of offspring (young).

buckthorn – a thorny tree or shrub having elliptic leaves and dark berries; considered an invasive species in Wisconsin.

burdock – a coarse, broad-leaved weed bearing prickly heads of burs that stick to the clothing; considered invasive in Wisconsin.

canopy – the uppermost layer in a forest, formed by the leafy "crowns" of the trees.

carapace – a bony or tough, protective, semitransparent shield or shell covering some or all of the dorsal part of an animal, as of a turtle.

carnivorous – eating meat.

chickadee – a small bird in the titmouse family, having the throat and top of the head black, with a distinctive "chicka-dee-dee-dee" call.

colleague – a person who works with you.

community outreach – an effort on the part of a helping organization (like a church, university, or the Urban Ecology Center) to provide information about its services to people in the neighborhood or larger community.

coyote – a wild, buff-gray, wolf-like member of the dog family, distinguished from the wolf by its relatively small size and its slender build, large ears, and narrow muzzle.

crayfish – any freshwater decapod (ten-footed) crustacean, closely related to but smaller than lobsters; also called crawdad, crawdaddy.

culture – a quality in a group of people that distinguishes them from another group of people.

damselfly – a slender, nonstinging insect of the order Odonata, distinguished from the dragonfly by having the wings folded back in line with the body when at rest.

data – fact, statistic, or item of information.

data entry – the job of typing text or other data onto a computer, as by typing on a keyboard or scanning a document.

deciduous – describing a tree or shrub that sheds its leaves annually.

decompress – to relax; unwind.

degraded area – an environment where nature has been altered so that plants and animals will not thrive there.

desolate – barren or laid waste; deprived of inhabitants; deserted; uninhabited.

dragonfly – a stout-bodied, non-stinging insect of the order Odonata, which preys on mosquitoes and other insects, and is distinguished from the damselfly by having wings outstretched rather than folded when at rest.

ecology – the branch of biology dealing with the relations and interactions between organisms and their environment, including other organisms.

eco-travel – traveling with the purpose of studying and enjoying an outdoor environment and the plants and animals within it.

embryo – the young of an animal in the early stages of development; also, the rudimentary plant usually contained in the seed.

embryonic – undeveloped, like a baby inside the womb.

ensue – to come afterward; to follow as a consequence; result.

environment – the air, water, minerals, organisms, and all other external factors surrounding us.

environmental ethic – moral principles or values held by people who want to take care of the environment.

environmental stewardship – the job of caring for the environment.

ephemeral wetland – a body of water lasting a very short time before drying out.

fox snake – a brown-blotched non-venomous snake that vibrates its tail and emits a pungent odor when disturbed.

fragile – easily broken, shattered, or damaged; delicate.

Freemason – a member of a widely distributed secret order, having for its object mutual assistance and the promotion of brotherly love among its members.

garlic mustard – a plant with edible leaves, small white flowers, and an odor of garlic; considered invasive in Wisconsin.

geologist – a scientist who studies the dynamics and physical history of the earth, its rocks, and the physical, chemical, and biological changes that the earth has undergone or is undergoing.

gopher tortoise – a burrowing (digging) tortoise, of the southeastern U.S.

goldenrod – composite plant usually bearing numerous small, yellow flower heads.

gravid – pregnant.

habitat – the natural environment of an organism; place that is natural for the life and growth of an organism.

habitat health – the state of balance in an environment, where plants and animals have adequate resources for life.

habitat management – the job of taking care of an environment so that it is healthy.

habitat restoration – the job of working to bring health and balance back to an environment that had become degraded; returning an environment to its origin with native plants and species.

igloo – a dome-shaped hut usually built of blocks of hard snow.

inclusivity – welcoming all people; not excluding participants on the grounds of gender, race, class, sexuality, disability, etc.

instar – an insect in any one of its periods of postembryonic growth between molts.

interconnectedness – being interrelated, interdependent; working together in cooperation.

intern – someone learning a job by doing it; similar to an apprentice; may be paid or unpaid.

interwebbing – being interconnected, dependent upon each other.

invasive species – plants or animals that aren't natural to an environment; often these species multiply rapidly, taking over so the native species are "squeezed out."

land stewardship – overseeing, protecting and preserving the environment in its natural state.

mammal surveys – counting and assessing the mammal species in a particular area; may include noting age, gender, condition, etc.

mangy – shabby, having hair loss.

maple sugaring – collecting sap from maple trees and cooking it down until it becomes sweet "maple syrup."

migratory - roving or nomadic, as in birds that fly south in autumn.

milkweed – a native Wisconsin pod-bearing plant that is essential for the lifecycle of the monarch butterfly.

native species – a plant or animal living in its normal place of origin.

natural progression – the normal way that a natural environment evolves, for instance changing over time from a lake to a swamp to a prairie to an oak savannah.

natural resources – the natural wealth of a country, consisting of land, forests, mineral deposits, water, air, etc.

nomadic - moving about from place to place; wandering.

northern shrike – a large songbird also known as a butcher bird.

oceanographer – one who studies and ocean, its geography, and all the life within it.

odenates – carnivorous insects including damselflies and dragonflies

organism – a form of life: animal, plant, fungus, etc.

oriole – a bird with prominent black and orange coloring. People often put out grape jelly and sugar water for orioles during spring migration.

ornithologist – one who studies birds.

perch – any place or object for a bird or animal to land or rest upon. Also, a type of small fish.

pellages – the coat or fur of an animal.

postembryonic – occurring after the embryonic phase.

recruitment – inviting others to join a certain group or organization.

research – the work of careful investigation into a subject in order to discover or revise facts, theories, etc.

resourceful – able to deal skillfully and promptly with new situations, difficulties, etc.; able to search and locate resources to help one deal with these things.

retention pond – an artificial pool of water that has vegetation around it, created for the purpose of controlling storm water runoff and preventing flooding into homes.

riprap – broken stone used to help hold earth embankments along rivers.

rookies – people who are new to any particular occupation, game, etc.

salamander – a tailed amphibian having soft, moist, scaleless skin, typically aquatic as a larva and semiterrestrial as an adult; several species are endangered.

sap – the juice or vital circulating fluid of a plant, especially of a woody plant.

savannah – a mixed woodland grassland ecosystem characterized by the trees being sufficiently widely spaced so that the canopy does not close.

scarlet tanager – a bird, the male of which is bright red with black wings and tail during the breeding season.

Schmeeckle Reserve – a 280-acre natural land area on the University of Wisconsin-Stevens Point.

semiterrestrial – living mostly on land but requiring a moist environment or nearby water, especially as a breeding site.

shrew – a small mole-like animal.

snapping turtle – a large freshwater turtle, having a large head and powerful hooked jaws.

soft opening – an opening to the public without much advertising, before a grand opening, so workers have a chance to smooth out details without huge crowds.

solar power – heat radiation from the sun converted into electrical power.

solstices – two times during the year when the sun is at its greatest distance from the celestial equator: about June 21 (summer solstice) or about December 22 (winter solstice).

species – in biology, regarded as the basic category of biological classification, composed of related individuals that resemble one another, are able to breed among themselves, but are not able to breed with members of another species.

speech therapy – treatment to improve the speech of children who have difficulty in learning to speak properly.

stereotype – a simplified and standardized idea or image that has special meaning and held in common by members of a group. For example, cowboys and Indians are American stereotypes.

sustainable – pertaining to a system that maintains itself by using techniques that allow for continual reuse. A sustainable system does not depend on other systems to keep it running.

symbiosis – the intimate association between two different organisms, often to the benefit of both.

restoration – bringing back an area to a former, original, or normal condition.

toxin – poisonous substance produced within living cells or organisms.

triglyceride – a component which is found in blood and helps to indicate the health of an organism

upland hardwood forest – a woods made up of shade tolerant, deciduous trees (sometimes with pines and evergreens), with an understory of wood shrubs and groundcover plants, generally located on elevated, rolling terrain such as slopes and bluffs.

venom – a toxin injected by an animal with stingers, fangs, etc.

vernal pond - a pool that dries periodically and doesn't support breeding populations of fish.

vole – a small rodent, relative of the mouse.

white cedar - a fragrant evergreen tree.

yellow-throated warbler - small migratory songbird species

RECOMMENDED READING

Leinbach, Ken, *Urban Ecology: A Natural Way to Transform Kids, Parks, Cities, and the World*

Louv, Richard, *Last Child in the Woods: Saving Our Children from Nature-Deficit Disorder*

Let us go, then, you and I,
feet soft upon the earth,
hearts open.

Gail Grenier

About Gail Grenier, Story Gatherer

Gail Grenier is a veteran journalist, teacher, activist and volunteer. She has received awards for her newspaper column and for her articles about vanishing farms and the environment. Since 1993, she has taught Creative Writing for Publication at Waukesha County Technical College. In 1982, she founded HOPE Network, a nonprofit agency serving families headed by single mothers in Greater Milwaukee. She continues to volunteer with HOPE.

The mother of three and grandmother of six, she lives with her husband, Michael Sweet, in Milwaukee, Wisconsin.

Blog: *Gail Grenier Here*
Her blog and books can be found through her website,
www.gailgreniersweet.com